ENDORSEMENTS

"As a public school teacher for ten years, Stephen Williams saw firsthand the challenges facing Christians in public schools, and he desires to equip parents to protect their children's faith and worldview. Weaving the story of the court case he was involved in makes the book intriguing on multiple levels."

Josh McDowell (www.Josh.org)
Author of *Evidence that Demands a Verdict* and *More Than a Carpenter*

"At a time when religious liberty is under attack from all sides, *Navigating Public Schools* is a much needed resource for parents, students, and teachers in public schools to remind them that they actually have robust Constitutional freedoms at school. Stephen's own story of how he courageously took a stand and victoriously asserted those freedoms in the face of intense opposition should serve as an inspiration for others across our country to do the same."

Gary McCaleb, J.D. Regent University
Senior Counsel and Executive Vice President, Alliance Defending Freedom
(www.ADFlegal.org)

"As a superintendent within the public school system, I want to see parents actively engage in the educational journey of their children and to feel they have a voice. Parents will benefit greatly from the guidance contained in *Navigating Public Schools*. This book provides important information on students' and parents' rights in schools, and also insights about how to properly handle conflict should it arise. As a parent, I also appreciated the encouragement to build a strong faith and worldview foundation at home. Families in the public school system will benefit greatly from owning and reading *Navigating Public Schools*."

Shay Mikalson
Public School District Superintendent

"*Navigating Public Schools* is a book whose time is come. It is clearly for such a time as this because, sadly—and many times, unintentionally—public school teachers and curricula are presented in such a way as to explicitly or implicitly undermine a Christian worldview. This book is overflowing with great, practical advice to parents who want to not only protect their children, but to empower them to live and think for Christ. Quite frankly, I cannot think of another book like this, and I highly endorse it."

J.P. Moreland, Ph.D.
Distinguished Professor of Philosophy, Biola University
Author of *Love Your God With All Your Mind*

"At this time in history when our public schools are often adversarial toward Christianity and intolerant of a Biblical worldview, it is imperative for all Christian educators and parents to read *Navigating Public Schools*. Stephen and Sarah Williams do a fantastic job of analyzing our public schools, past and present, while emphasizing the importance of not sacrificing our Biblical worldview nor that of our children."

Finn Laursen

Executive Director, Christian Educators Association International (www.ceai.org)

"Stephen and Sarah Williams have done us all a great service by producing such a thoughtful and carefully researched book to guide us through the American public school system. They are uniquely qualified to do this with tremendous wisdom and expertise. This book needs to be in the hands of every caring Christian parent in the country."

Craig J. Hazen, Ph.D.

Founder and Director, Christian Apologetics graduate program, Biola University
Author of the novel *Five Sacred Crossings*

"Stephen and Sarah Williams have written a book that will greatly help students, parents, teachers, and all school staff to navigate the murky waters of public education as it relates to Christianity. I highly recommend equipping yourself with the insight and knowledge they provide in *Navigating Public Schools*—I only wish this book had been available when I was a teacher and principal in public schools."

Dane Danforth

Public School Teacher and Principal for 19 years

"This book will empower Christian teachers, parents, and students to navigate the often turbulent waters of our public schools. *Navigating Public Schools* doesn't enter into the debate about whether or not Christian students should be in public schools. It recognizes the fact that the majority of Christian kids *are* in public schools and so need to be discerning about what they are taught. Anyone involved in public schools—including staff, volunteers, extra-curricular groups, and all who are hungry for guidance on the journey—will find this book helpful. It clarifies what rights Christians have in the school system and how we can exercise those rights in a loving, yet effective, way."

Eric Buehrer

President, Gateways to Better Education (www.gtbe.org)

"Most of us, as Christian parents, have an increasing concern about the world our children will inherit and the nature of the public school system that will prepare many of them for their journey through life. Stephen and Sarah Williams have done all of us a service in *Navigating Public Schools*. They provide unique insight into the challenges of the public school environment along with a thoughtful framework to equip our young people for success."

J. **Warner Wallace**, Cold-Case Detective
Author of *Cold-Case Christianity* and *God's Crime Scene*

"In 2004, many in our land of liberty were stunned to read headlines like 'Declaration of Independence Banned in Cupertino California.' Stephen Williams was in the eye of the storm of protest that was caused by his teaching that the founding of America was expressed in terms of faith in God. In fact, the importance of God for our Founders is inescapably evident when the four direct references to deity are identified in our Declaration. Based upon his remarkable experiences emanating from that tumultuous time, Stephen and Sarah have written a wise, readable and commendable handbook for families entitled, *Navigating Public Schools*. I encourage you to read this book for wisdom and guidance, as well as for assessing the seemingly inexorable march of American culture toward the establishment of non-theistic secular ideology as the American creed."

Dr. Peter A. Lillback, President, The Providence Forum
Author of *George Washington's Sacred Fire*

"From the perspective of being teachers and coaches, we see the powerful influences vying for the hearts and minds of our youth. *Navigating Public Schools* provides critical information for Christians to stand strong in a raging sea of ideas. We must be proactive in teaching our children the defense of their faith, so they will recognize ideology contrary to a Biblical worldview. Stephen and Sarah provide excellent information and resources Christians must know to impact their communities, schools, and homes in both an effective and respectful way."

Kent Wieber, Public School Teacher, Social Studies Chair and Coach
Heather Wieber, Public School Teacher and Coach

"Stephen and Sarah Williams have done a remarkable job to help any reader understand the importance of a Biblical worldview in a culture becoming more secular every year. They give a clear historical overview how our culture shifted from a Judeo-Christian worldview to a secular view. His personal legal journey through this clash between Christian and secular as a Christian teacher in a public school makes reading the book come alive. They clarify terms, explain ideas, give answers and provide solutions to people searching for guidance. They do this by providing an accurate understanding of the concept of the separation of church and state. They clarify people's rights as Christians involved in public schools, coaching or leadership as well as parenting. A great resource book for Christians living in a modern world."

Larry Day, Ph.D. Psychology, Studied at L'Abri under Dr. Francis Schaefer
Author of *Self-Esteem by God's Design*

"This is a must-read book for all parents, children, and teachers trying to figure out how to stay true to Jesus Christ while working within the secular U.S. public school system. Stephen Williams knows what he's talking about, having made national headlines when his school principal banned Stephen's teaching of the Declaration of Independence in his classroom. Stephen and Sarah Williams write as a team, and their writing is winsome, practical, and full of wise counsel. They show the reader how to navigate the turbulent waters of teaching about God and living the Christian life in today's secular public school setting. This book will save you a lot of worry and grief, while giving you the confidence to know and defend your God-given rights and beliefs."

Joel Comiskey, Ph.D. Fuller Seminary
Founder of Joel Comiskey Group (www.joelcomiskeygroup.com)
Author of *Planting Churches that Reproduce*

"We thank God for the ministry that Stephen and Sarah have devoted their lives to all these years. Their devotion to God's truth, and their love for others, is a true testimony . . . Stephen and Sarah have taken great care to gracefully provide powerful insights that offer the reader hope and wisdom in the midst of the raging war of ideas within our public school system."

Jason Jimenez and Alex McFarland of the StandStrongTour.com
Jason Jimenez, Founder/Director of Re|Shift Ministries (www.ReShiftMinistries.org)
Author of *The Raging War of Ideas: How to Take Back Our Faith, Family, and Country*
Alex McFarland, Director of AlexMcFarland.com
Author of *The 10 Most Common Objections to Christianity—and How To Answer Them*

"*Navigating Public Schools* is a breath of life-giving oxygen . . . A vital text for all Christians engaged in the public education system (and anyone wanting to understand it) that draws upon common sense, original texts, and the American legal code. Serving as a guiding light in the dark hallways of our (all too-often) anti-Christian public schools, the Williamses provide easily understandable and eminently usable material for us all."

Rev. Timothy Sternberg, M.Div., M.S. Ed.
Author of *Fear Not, I Am with You!*

"As the Director of the Greater Portland Area Chapter of Child Evangelism Fellowship, I highly recommend *Navigating Public Schools* by my friends Stephen and Sarah Williams. This book is an excellent resource for all Christians involved in the public education system, including those called to work in Christian clubs or groups. The guidance and practical tools in this book will help keep the gospel of Jesus Christ alive within our public school system."

Ron Imig
Portland, Oregon Area Director, Child Evangelism Fellowship

"As a newsman, I well remember Stephen Williams' 'church-state separation' case . . . Now, after a decade of mapping out public education's increasingly hazardous terrain, Stephen and his wife, Sarah, have written a valuable, heartfelt and highly practical primer to help Christian families involved in the public school system."

> **David Kupelian**, Managing Editor of WND.com
> Author of *The Marketing of Evil*

"*Navigating Public Schools* encouraged me tremendously as a teacher in public school. By gaining a better understanding of my legal rights in the public school system, I no longer feel like I am walking on a tightrope in regards to what I can and cannot say regarding my faith. I also have a better grasp on the fact that schools are not meant to be "religion-free zones," according to the Supreme Court. I would highly recommend this book to all Christian teachers and staff involved in the public school system. You will be greatly encouraged!"

> **Anthony Parla**
> Public School Teacher

"Stephen and Sarah are well respected throughout Central Oregon. Their acumen regarding public schools and Christian apologetics has helped hundreds of young people, parents, and teachers by giving them the longitudes and latitudes, so to speak, that steer them clear of dangerous secular reefs. I would encourage anyone involved in the public school system to read *Navigating Public Schools*."

> **Ken Johnson**
> Pastor, Westside Church, Bend, Oregon
> Author of *Life*

"This book is a must read for believers whose children attend public schools. Stephen and Sarah skillfully acquaint the reader with the spiritual condition of our public schools, the challenges, the rights available to parents, and most importantly, how to navigate through the trials encountered while we strive to raise our children according to a Christian worldview."

> **Rex Smith**
> Chairman: Board of Trustees, Western Seminary, Retired Silicon Valley Executive

"Stephen and Sarah Williams have developed a tremendous resource for potentially millions of Christian families. As both a father and grandfather, I know our own family has faced the full range of schooling choices and challenges. This new book is a well-researched, thorough guide for those whose children are in public schools. And because that is the reality for so many Christian families, the help and encouragement offered by the Williamses is both practical and critical."

> **John Fortmeyer**
> Publisher, *Christian News Northwest* newspaper

NAVIGATING PUBLIC SCHOOLS

CHARTING A COURSE TO PROTECT YOUR CHILD'S
CHRISTIAN FAITH AND WORLDVIEW

Rev. Stephen John Williams

Sarah Middleton Williams, Ph.D.

PREPARE THE WAY
PUBLISHING

www.PrepareTheWay.us

LCCN: 2016932251
ISBN: 978-0-9971419-0-0

Prepare the Way Publishing LLC is the book and resource publishing division
of Prepare the Way Ministries. Our mission is to equip and empower Christians
to uphold a Biblical worldview and influence our culture for Christ.
www.PrepareTheWay.us

Editing by J.P. Brooks and Lynn Pollack
Interior layout by Greg Johnson, Textbook Perfect
Cover design by Derek Thornton

Printed in the United States of America.

ACKNOWLEDGMENTS

First and foremost, we want to thank God for His amazing grace and love. I (Stephen) want to thank my Lord and Savior, Jesus Christ, for loving and rescuing me, a hard-hearted atheist, in 2001. I (Sarah) wish to thank those who have served in campus ministry at the University of Michigan, Oxford, and Stanford, who helped me answer Jesus's most important question: "Who do you say that I am?"

There are many people who have been instrumental in helping this book come to fruition. Our four daughters, Maggie, Elizabeth, Rebekah, and Mary Catherine, have had abundant patience with us through the process. We have cherished the faithful intercessory prayers of many friends and family over the years. We could not have finished this book without those who have partnered with Prepare the Way Ministries and believed in the work God called us to. Joel Comiskey's invaluable guidance kept us on track. J.P. Brooks provided excellent editing help at the perfect time. Finally, Alliance Defending Freedom provided free legal help during the federal court case; their staff was a great encouragement.

CONTENTS

Foreword by Sean McDowell 13

Authors' Note 15

Introduction 16

Chapter 1   Study the Map 20

Chapter 2   Understand the Prevailing Winds. 28

Chapter 3   Who Is Your Family's Anchor? 50

Chapter 4   Join the Armada: Don't Journey Alone 60

Chapter 5   The "Separation of Church and State" Shipwreck. 68

Chapter 6   Take the Ship's Wheel: Know Your Rights 82

Chapter 7   Chart Your Course: Prepare for Curriculum
Issues—History/Social Studies 111

Chapter 8   Chart Your Course: Prepare for Curriculum
Issues—Science 129

Chapter 9   Chart Your Course: Prepare for Curriculum
Issues—Literature/Sex Education/Anti-Bullying/
Holidays/Common Core 147

Chapter 10   Keep Watch for Worldview Pirates 162

Chapter 11   When Conflict is Necessary, Signal for Help. 177

Chapter 12   Raising Our Flag: Influencing Our Schools for Christ. . . . 190

Appendix A   Religious Expression in Public Schools
(U.S. Secretary of Education). 205

Appendix B   Guidance on Constitutionally Protected Prayer
and Religious Expression in Public Schools
(U.S. Department of Education) 207

Appendix C   Rights of Students and Religious Clubs on Campus 209

Appendix D   The Free Speech and Academic Freedom of
Teachers in Public Schools. 214

Appendix E   Further Resources on Rights in the Public
School System 217

Appendix F   Declaration of Independence 218

Appendix G   Preamble and Bill of Rights of the U.S. Constitution 223

About the Authors 226

FOREWORD

As a high school teacher for many years, and now as a college professor, I have been acutely aware that Christian students face mounting challenges to their faith and worldview from our increasingly secular culture. It has been my experience that few students are ready for these challenges. And many parents do not feel ready either! They long to help their children stand firm in the faith, but it can be a daunting task these days. Many Christian parents often wonder, "Where do I start?"

The good news is that we Christians have more resources than ever to help parents and students recognize the key worldview tensions in our culture and answer the tough questions of the faith. I have devoted much of my life and ministry trying to help students answer these hard questions and to prepare them for the challenges they will face. But sometimes the trick is figuring out just where to start. I appreciate this new resource, *Navigating Public Schools*, written by my friends Stephen and Sarah Williams, because it serves as an excellent starting point to help parents effectively equip their children with a biblical worldview. Preparation is key—the earlier we can build a firm foundation as a family, the better able we are to navigate challenges along the journey.

Public schools have become increasingly secular environments with unique challenges for Christians. Parents navigating the public school system will likely face significant challenges to their faith, yet there are surprisingly few resources directed specifically towards families within public school settings. This book illuminates some of the major worldview, social, relational, and curriculum issues the younger generation faces in schools today. More importantly, it points parents in the right direction to get a hold of the best resources. And it accomplishes this with seriousness and urgency, but without overreaction.

I highly recommend this book, which covers a wide range of important topics for those navigating public schools, from worldview equipping to becoming excellent ambassadors for Christ to cultivating strong relationships with children. It is not overwhelming, but guides parents in a stepwise fashion. This book is ideal for busy parents who want clear tools to navigate curriculum pitfalls, exercise their parental rights in schools, and build a strong worldview foundation as a family. It is a must-have for parents with children in the public school system.

I am grateful for the research and efforts the Williamses have put into this book. It comes from their personal journey, insights, and firsthand work with the next generation. Even though I currently send my kids to a Christian school, I grew up going to a public school (along with my three sisters). Things turned out well for us, but it didn't happen by accident. My parents were actively involved in my education and took the kind of advice offered here. If you are willing to take advantage of this resource, and put its advice into action, you too can be empowered to raise up your kids successfully through public schools. Enjoy!

Sean McDowell, Ph.D. (www.SeanMcDowell.org)
Professor of Christian Apologetics, Biola University
Author of *A New Kind of Apologist*

Authors' Note

This book is a joint labor of love, concern, prayer, and ministry. Because Stephen happens to be the one of us who was the public school teacher for ten years, the majority of our book is written from his perspective and his first-hand knowledge. Therefore, except where noted otherwise, "I" refers to him.

We hope that this book is a resource that readers can continually refer to through the course of their educational journey. Note that you will find several useful documents in the appendices including the rights of students, teachers, and staff. On Prepare the Way Ministries' website (www.PrepareTheWay.us), there are multiple documents that you can download for free on topics such as The Reliability of the Bible, Evidence for Christianity, United States' Christian Heritage, Science and Christianity, Rights of Christians and many others.

INTRODUCTION

I found myself on my knees late one night, moved to tears and crying out to God for help. I had dimmed the light so as not to wake my pregnant wife. My one-year-old daughter periodically let out a muffled little "coo."

It was not a convenient time, to say the least, for my wife and me to become involved in a federal court battle, nor in the accompanying nationwide media frenzy and public controversy. Not only did I have a young family, but I was in the middle of growing my teaching career.

Then again, life does not always cater to us or to our convenience. So the headlines about me were rolling off the press almost daily . . . from the *New York Times, Los Angeles Times, San Francisco Chronicle, San Jose Mercury*, and many others. The "little" case I had filed with the help of the Alliance Defending Freedom just prior to Thanksgiving of 2004 had somehow snowballed out of control.

"Who could be calling us so early?" my wife had asked when our phone rang at 6 AM on that first Saturday after the filing. We knew that our lives had changed drastically when I picked up the phone and heard these words:

"This is *Good Morning America*, and we'd like to fly you out to New York to have you on the show tomorrow to talk about your court case."

As I discuss in greater detail later in this book, throughout the 2003–2005 school years my principal had prevented me from using primary-source historical documents from America's founding—simply because they sometimes mentioned God, the Bible, or Christianity. A parent of one of my students was a confrontational atheist, and this parent would not tolerate any mention of God in the classroom, not even when the discussion was completely in line with the state's curriculum standards. But after my principal banned my lesson on the Declaration of Independence, I felt forced to take action. So I prayed with my wife and others, talked with attorneys at the Alliance Defending Freedom, and felt led to file a complaint in federal court.

What I had not considered was how my decision would affect my family. When the media started calling us, however, I realized that my simple little case had—to quote Sean Hannity, who inter-viewed me—"ignited a debate in the nation."

Soon after the case escalated in the media, some friends cautioned me about some parents in my school district who were extremely upset about the district getting such massive negative publicity. This publicity, of course, could lower these parents' property values (as they discussed in their online communica-tions). Some friends were monitoring the online public discussion groups these parents had started, and some of these parents were hinting at a willingness to lie and slander me in unthinkable ways. I knew when I started the case that I had signed up for an incon-venience, but I had not imagined the possibility that my family would be at the mercy of such malicious people.

And so I found myself on my knees that night, crying out to the Lord, praying for His wisdom and guidance and protection for my family. Fortunately, I was not alone. My wife joined me in prayer that night and stood by me throughout our ordeal.

In spite of my fervent prayers, I was almost ready to drop the case completely. But while I had been praying, God had been working. Later that very morning He used my class "room mom" in an amazing way to greatly encourage me. (You can read the whole story in Chapter 12.) God used this unforgettable experi-ence of His presence and support to give me an abundant peace and trust in Him: a trust that He was in charge of my case, and that He would use it for His purposes.

After the case was settled, I believed one of God's purposes was to direct me towards full-time ministry, so I could help other Christians who found themselves in similar situations to mine. So many parents and friends I had talked to were baffled about what to do in the face of official opposition to their faith in the public arena. Many were huddled under the proverbial bowl (Matthew 5:15). "Well, *is* it okay to use William Penn's *Frame of Government* in a public school? It does have a lot of Christian ref-erences," one friend said to me. Even bold Christians who taught in public schools and colleges described their feelings of walking a tightrope: any mention of Christianity, and down you fall. The secular culture kindles fears of lawsuits by the ACLU, and job loss, and awkward labels of "fundamentalist fanatic" among your workplace colleagues. Many non-Christians in the media and the educational establishment peddle the fear that you are playing with fire if you mention anything overtly Christian in the classroom or curriculum. The result? All too often, we have an illegal and un-Constitutional hostility towards Christianity in the public sphere.

So I resigned from my teaching job to start Prepare the Way Ministries. The mission of Prepare the Way is to equip Christians to stand firm in their faith and empower them to uphold a Biblical worldview in an increasingly secular culture. One facet of our ministry is to help Christians navigate the public school system. This book is an extension of that mission. Romans 8:28 says that God works all things for the good for those who love Him and are called according to His purposes. I pray that this book will be one of the good things that emerged from a tough battle.

The goal of this book is to encourage and equip Christians who, after earnest prayer, decide to place their children in the public school system. We cannot stress too strongly the importance of Christians praying about whether to educate their children in a secular, Christian, or homeschool environment. We are not advocating that you place your kids in public schools, and we are not advocating that you take them out. We *are* encouraging you to make an informed and prayerful decision, being aware of the dangers that your children will most likely face in public schools. Then, if you still feel the Lord leading you to place them in the public school system, this book will hopefully be an invaluable resource as you set sail on the tumultuous seas that are the American public education system.

The stakes are high. Ultimately what we are talking about is the faith and worldview of the next generation of American Christians. What will they think of the Bible? Will it morph into merely some kind of spiritual "accessory" for them, or will they still consider it the inspired Word of God? What kind of world will they choose to shape? What kind of parents will they be? As Nancy Pearcey describes in her book *Total Truth*:

> As Christian parents, pastors, teachers, and youth group leaders, we constantly see young people pulled down by the undertow of powerful cultural trends. If all we give them is a "heart" religion, it will not be strong enough to counter the lure of attractive but dangerous ideas. Young believers also need a

"brain" religion—training in worldview and apologetics—to equip them to analyze and critique the competing worldviews they will encounter when they leave home. If forewarned and forearmed, young people at least have a fighting chance when they find themselves a minority of one among their classmates or work colleagues. Training young people to develop a Christian mind is no longer an option; it is part of their necessary survival equipment.[1]

You might sense some measure of urgency in this book. This is because we parents do not have much time with our young people before they leave home. For almost ten years now, Prepare the Way Ministries has been organizing a conference called the Christian Youth Summit; the mission of this conference is to help equip students with a Biblical worldview before they leave home. We often hear amazing testimonies of spiritual awakening and transformation that happened at the Summit. We also observe a troubling trend: many of our Christian young people feel neither "forewarned" nor "forearmed" for the kind of world they are entering. Their world is not a zero-entry pool, but a drop-off into a vast sea of secularism. And study after study shows that our Christian young people are not prepared to swim in it.

Our hope and prayer is that this book will serve as a tool and resource for thousands of parents and caring adults, to help them be intentional about forewarning and forearming our youth. As parents of four children ourselves, Sarah and I understand parental fatigue. Yet we all need to rise to this occasion; we need to draw on the energy of the Christian community and band together in our crucial mission of raising children who have a vibrant faith and a clear Christian worldview. Although this book is geared toward parents, it is intended for all Christians who are affiliated with the American public school system in any way. It contains invaluable information for teachers, staff, volunteers, teachers aides, administrators, extra-curricular Christian club leaders, pastors, grandparents, and others. The more informed and equipped *all* Christians involved in public schools are, the better.

Study the map. Fight apathy. Trust God to guide you.

---

[1] Nancy Pearcey, *Total Truth: Liberating Christianity from Its Cultural Captivity*, Crossway Books, 2004, p.19

CHAPTER 1

STUDY THE MAP

It was a typical sunny afternoon in Cupertino, California. The bell had just rung and the school day was over when the principal briskly walked into my room. She looked very concerned. The minute she walked through the door, I knew something was wrong. Her expression was in stark contrast to the playful atmosphere of my thirty-two laughing 5th-graders parading out the door. I said hello and asked how she was doing. Skipping all pleasantries, she cut to the chase.

"What were you doing talking about God in class today?" she asked.

I was taken off guard. My mind thought back to what we had done that day in class . . . there had been nothing noteworthy, or so I thought.

Then I remember that just after the pledge of allegiance earlier that morning, a student had asked me why we say "under God" in the pledge. It was September of 2003 and the Supreme Court was going to be hearing the Michael Newdow case on this exact topic.[2] Including the words "under God" in the pledge of allegiance had been ruled un-Constitutional by a Ninth Circuit Court of Appeals, and headlines were buzzing with debate. We periodically discussed current events in the classroom, so it was reasonable to answer the student's question. I asked the class what they thought, and they had a short discussion on the topic. I had

---

[2] http://www.christianpost.com/news/atheist-newdow-says-legal-fight-against -under-god-is-over-49549/

remained neutral while facilitating their dialogue. After a few minutes, we moved on to math.

I explained the scenario to my principal. Though she looked at me a bit suspiciously, she said it sounded reasonable. She went on to explain that an anonymous parent had called in and complained that I was teaching their child about God. "Be careful," she warned.

As I drove home that night, I reflected on my previous years at Stevens Creek Elementary School. As a veteran public school teacher, I was very careful to honor the policies not to proselytize in the classroom. At the same time, I did not want to fall into the trap of being ashamed of my Christian faith. I attended a staff Bible study that met after school hours, regularly chatted with a mother's prayer group, and was beginning to help some parents start an after-school Christian club. I knew that some staff members and parents labeled me as "the Christian guy" because of my involvement with the campus Christian community. However, this was the first time I had ever received a complaint about it. I suspected that the anonymous parent had known about my Christian faith and did not want her child in my class. Little did I know that this complaint was the first domino in a series of events that would result in a federal court case and radically change my faith, family, and career.

Stories like mine are becoming all too common.[3] Schools are becoming increasingly secularized and even hostile to the Christian faith. Some teachers have told students not to read their Bibles during free reading time (though it is legal to do so). Students may experience resistance when attempting to start a Christian club, though numerous other clubs meet freely and receive school funds. We have counseled students who have been called "ignorant" by their teachers simply for voicing their belief in Christianity. The peer pressure that students face daily in schools often goes directly against the Biblical guidance that parents attempt to impress upon them. Many students end up feeling ashamed of their faith, and their Christian worldview slowly erodes.

---

[3] http://www.crosswalk.com/blogs/dr-james-emery-white/are-christians-in -america-under-attack.html

What do children learn at school? They learn much more than simply academic subjects. They learn about life. They learn about the world. If your child attends public schools, they likely spend more waking hours there than in your home. Given the influence of teachers and coaches, friends and peers, and the hours spent doing homework, it is clear that school will play a large role in shaping your child's worldview and their faith.

For Christians, navigating the public school system is becoming increasingly daunting. Christian parents often feel anxiety about sending their children into the public school environment. This book is meant to help Christian parents navigate the public school system and be intentional about charting a course to protect their child's faith and Biblical worldview. In addition, this book will be a useful resource for teachers, administrators, volunteers, and anyone involved in the public school system.

STUDY THE BIBLICAL MAP

If you were to set out tomorrow to sail across the ocean in a small boat, wouldn't it be wise to consult a map? The seas might look peaceful and inviting at first, but where are the coral reefs? Where are the currents and the safe havens? Where exactly are you going, and what is the best route to take? Thank God that He does not leave us without a map for our journey through life.

The Bible states very clearly that as Christian parents, the most important goal of our parenting journey is to pass the torch of faith to our children. Deuteronomy 6:5–7 says,

> Love the Lord your God with all your heart and with all your soul and with all your strength. These commandments that I give you today are to be on your hearts. *Impress them on your children.* Talk about them when you sit at home and when you walk along the road, when you lie down and when you get up. [emphasis added]

Israel constantly got into trouble for failing to pass their devotion to God on to the next generation, ultimately with disastrous consequences. Reading verses about children and parenting in the Bible, it's clear that God wants us to be intentional about passing the faith on to our children. Yet so many parents have not estab-lished solid spiritual goals for their family. We may be concerned, even anxious, about whether our children will stick with the faith, but frequently our daily focus is on their grades, sports, friends, schedules, and the general busyness that is rampant in our culture.

Our early years as parents are consumed by meeting the physical needs of our babies and toddlers. As our children get older, we are faced with a more daunting task: shepherding them on a spiritual journey through the formative and critical years of growing up. I heard a pastor say recently that children are empty vessels with wide-open hearts and minds, waiting for you to fill them. The world will try to fill them with all sorts of things. Our job is to fill their hearts and minds with a Christian worldview: the truth of God's love for them, His plan of salvation, His purposes in using their gifts for His kingdom. Proverbs 22:6 says, "Train a child in the way he should go, and when he is old he will not turn from it." Proverbs are wise teachings; the wisdom packed in this verse is that it is our job as adults to train children in the faith. Parents are exhorted to train children in a Biblical worldview, both in the Old and New Testaments. In First Timothy 4, the Apostle Paul says this (italics added): "*Train* yourself to be godly. For phys-ical training is of some value, but godliness has value for all things, holding promise for both the present life and the life to come." The Greek word Paul used for "train" is *goom-nad'-zo* (to exercise vigorously, in any way, either the body or the mind). The context here is serious training, like training for the Olympics or studying to be a doctor.

All Christians are called to this type of training, and it does not happen merely by going to church once a week. We must start with ourselves, letting God transform us on a daily basis. Then we are called to "train" our children. This type of training is not simply going to happen—not even by sending our kids to Sunday school and forcing them to go to church when they don't want to. This is training that is thought out and intentional. This is our highest calling as parents.

Our parenting "map"—the Bible—warns us that there will be obstacles in our path. This should be no surprise to us. I am sure we have all experienced many difficult hurdles in life. But God graciously points out many of the key obstacles. One scriptural illustration is found in the Parable of the Sower, in Matthew 13:18–23 (ESV). There Jesus explains the four types of soil:

> Hear then the parable of the sower: When anyone hears the word of the kingdom and does not understand it, the evil one comes and snatches away what has been sown in his heart. This is what was sown along the path. As for what was sown on rocky ground, this is the one who hears the word and immediately receives it with joy, yet he has no root in himself, but endures for a while, and when tribulation or persecution arises on account of the word, immediately he falls away. As for what was sown among thorns, this is the one who hears the word, but the cares of the world and the deceitfulness of riches choke the word, and it proves unfruitful. As for what was sown on good soil, this is the one who hears the word and understands it. He indeed bears fruit and yields, in one case a hundredfold, in another sixty, and in another thirty.

It is our job as parents to train up our children (and ourselves) so that our families are "good soil" and will not be led astray from the faith. According to the parable, some who fall away lack an understanding of the Gospel, some are unprepared for persecution, others are distracted by the cares and pleasures of the world. The key stumbling blocks revealed in this teaching from Jesus are obvious, yet how many families truly prepare to overcome these obstacles? As parents, we must not only be able to model a true *relationship* with Christ; we must also have a solid Biblical worldview that we must pass on to our children.

STUDY THE CULTURAL MAP

Studying the cultural map can be a bit daunting these days. How are Christians doing in passing the torch of faith to the next generation?[4] Sadly, the statistics show that roughly 50–70% of teens raised in Bible-believing homes walk away from their faith when they leave home.[5] After years of research, David Kinnaman of the Barna Group recently said in his book *You Lost Me*: "Young

---

[4] http://coldcasechristianity.com/2015/are-young-people-really-leaving-christianity/
[5] https://www.barna.org/barna-update/family-kids

people are skeptical about the reliability of the original Biblical manuscripts; they tend to read the Bible through a lens of pluralism . . . the theological foundations of even the most faithful young believers seem, in some crucial ways, shaky or unreliable."[6]

Not only are young people abandoning their faith in alarming numbers, but it appears that many do not even completely grasp the key tenets of the faith to begin with. In short, many do not truly understand the faith that they claim to reject. This is not too surprising considering that even adult Christians are confused about their worldview. Research shows what many consider to be a worldview crisis among Christians. A nationwide survey determined that only four percent of Americans have a Biblical worldview. More shocking, the results for self-professing "born-again" believers in America were *a dismal nineteen percent*.[7] You might ask, "What constitutes a Biblical worldview?" Maybe there were some complex questions about Biblical theology? No such excuse. Here is a list of the eight Yes-or-No questions that Barna asked the sample group:

- Do absolute moral truths exist?
- Is absolute truth defined by the Bible?
- Did Jesus Christ live a sinless life?
- Is God the all-powerful and all-knowing Creator of the universe, and does He still rule it today?
- Is salvation a gift from God that cannot be earned?
- Is Satan real?
- Does a Christian have a responsibility to share his or her faith in Christ with other people?
- Is the Bible accurate in all of its teachings?

The Bible's answers to these questions are considered core doctrines of Christianity. This survey revealed just how much secularization has occurred, even among those who consider themselves Christian.

---

[6] David Kinnaman, *You Lost Me*, Baker Books, 2011
[7] Barna Research Group, 2003

When we study the cultural map of present-day America, it seems clear that parents, children, and the Christian faith community as a whole are not navigating the cultural obstacles very effectively. Many Christian leaders and scholars have different theories about why this is the case. I am not arguing that public schools are the primary reason. However, I believe the fact that *most* Christian kids spend *most* of their time in a public school environment is an important contributing factor. I base this on ten years of teaching in the public school system. My goal is not to debate whether children should be in public schools or Christian schools or home schooled. Many other ministries explore these issues. The fact is that the majority of Christian kids *are* in public schools today. We hope that parents make this decision intentionally and prayerfully.

Christian parents, kids, teachers, administrators, volunteers, and youth workers who have chosen to be involved in the public school system are hungry for resources to help them navigate more effectively. They need help, because the powerful winds, treacherous currents, and dangerous shoals (shallow places) along their journey are numerous. Many kids are exhausted by the journey, and so are their parents. It can be discouraging to meet countless Christians who feel far off course.

Our purpose in writing this book is to see parents, children, and caring adults emerge from a state of denial or powerlessness and take action in upholding the right to express a Biblical worldview in public schools. Our mission is to train Christians to be "sailing masters" on their journey across the ocean of the public school system.

The term "sailing master" is a historic term for a naval officer trained in and responsible for the navigation of a sailing ship. This title showed that the sailor was a professional seaman and a specialist in navigation. We long to meet more Christian "sailing masters" in the public school system. These individuals and families know what they believe and why they believe it. They are confident in their faith. They are prepared for the stumbling blocks they will encounter on the journey. If you have met one of these students or families, you know how refreshing they are and how much hope they bring to our culture. Their children will be leaders in carrying the torch of faith to the next generation.

WHERE DO YOU WANT TO GO AS A FAMILY?

For many parents, it is empowering to pause and think about this question: *What are the spiritual goals for my family?* The Great Commission in Matthew 28 says that we ought to make disciples and teach them to obey everything Jesus has commanded. Surely as parents our first missionary field is our home, and we need to make strong disciples of our children. We ought to equip them for their life journey and make sure we do everything we can to prevent their faith from slowly eroding away. Clearly this is part of the discipleship process. In today's culture, it can be a formidable task to cultivate strong relationships with our children and to help shape and protect their worldview. Thankfully, there are many encouraging tools and resources out there; you might be surprised at just how many. You have far more rights in our society than you might think, and you can maximize your influence on your kids by being intentional about the journey.

As you read this book, I pray that God will show you how to take action in helping you and your children stand firm and become sailing masters in the tumultuous waters of today's public schools. Some of you are still making choices about your kids' schooling and are praying for direction on whether to choose public, private, or home school. I pray that this book will give you insight as you ask God for wisdom on how best to educate your children.

I hope you will also find encouragement in this book. Some of you may be at a discouraging point in your journey. I have talked to many parents who are in that place where everything seems hopeless. Take heart: we have a God who longs to encourage us and who is "able to do far more than we can ask or imagine!"

Regardless of your situation, I pray that God will give you an even more caring heart for your children, that you would grasp more clearly the attacks they face and have compassion on them. I pray that you will realize more fully that they are worth fighting for, as they are the future of your family as well as tomorrow's leaders in the Church and in our culture.

CHAPTER 2

UNDERSTAND THE PREVAILING WINDS

The Christian religion is the most important and one of the first things in which all children, under a free government, ought to be instructed. . . . No truth is more evident to my mind than that the Christian religion must be the basis of any government intended to secure the rights and privileges of a free people.

—Noah Webster (1828)

The battle for humankind's future must be waged and won in the public school classroom by teachers who correctly perceive their role as the proselytizers of a new faith: A religion of humanity—utilizing a classroom instead of a pulpit to carry humanist values into wherever they teach. The classroom must and will become an arena of conflict between the old and the new—the rotting corpse of Christianity, together with its adjacent evils and misery, and the new faith of humanism.

—John J. Dunphy, *The Humanist* (1983)

Roughly 85% of children in America attend public schools.[1] On average they are in school 35 hours per week; this is roughly 1,400 hours per year. As a result, public schools have an enormous effect on the moral character and worldview of our children, and consequently on our nation. Most often, our children will be taught

---

[1] http://www.conservapedia.com/Public_schools_in_the_United_States

from a secular worldview. I have a lot of respect for teachers and administrators, especially those Christians who are constantly trying to balance being a Christian in a mostly secular environment. We have a responsibility to show respect to their efforts. That being said, I cannot mince words. My experience compels me to believe there is a worldview battle going on in the public schools and we have a responsibility to understand the history and current nature of that battle. Caught in the middle of this tug-of-war are the minds of the next generation.

Left to the prevailing cultural and intellectual winds in the public school system, most ships (students and parents) that set sail there will be blown along a secular course. If you are a parent, your job is to understand the prevailing winds and then work to stay on course to help your kids have a thriving faith. If you are a teacher or staff person in a public school environment, your challenge is to know your rights and not be ashamed of your faith. If you are someone who simply cares about the future generation, you might work towards empowering students in public schools to stand firm in their faith. The goal of this book is to help all of you become sailing masters.

The Winds of the Past

When I filed the federal court case that dealt with censorship of primary source documents with Christian references, my wife and I got a lot of media attention (much to her dismay) in the *San Francisco Chronicle*, the *New York Times*, the *Los Angeles Times*, and many more publications.[2] To sum it up, what I heard from the liberal media quite often went along these lines: "Those crazy evangelicals are at it again. They are trying to take over our school system by pushing their Christian agenda!"

Such statements are ironic, to say the least. They show that many people (even intelligent and knowledgeable people) have forgotten their American history. Christians are not trying to force their agenda in public spheres. Christians are simply trying

---

[2] Stephen J. Williams v. Patricia Vidmar, Cupertino Union School District et al, Case No. 04-4946, 11/22/2004

to *regain* their freedom to publicly exercise their faith, a freedom that has been eroded in the past fifty or so years. Incorporating primary source documents with Christian references into the curriculum is *not* proselytizing. These documents are part of our country's history, which includes a strong Judeo-Christian moral influence.

Understanding our country's history can also help empower Christians to shed some of the sheepish tendencies that are so prevalent. We must realize that our request for schools to respect a Christian worldview is not us promoting some right-wing evangelical plot. We have a rich Christian heritage in our nation, a heritage that the Founders wrote extensively about protecting. Understanding America's history helps us make wise assessments about the current state of affairs. After all, it was Thomas Jefferson who said, in 1784:

> History, by apprising them [the citizens], of the past will enable
> them to judge of the future; it will avail them of the experience
> of other times and other nations; it will qualify them as judges
> of the actions and designs of men.[3]

We must also realize that the opposite is true. When we do not know our history, we are easily deceived. Karl Marx noted, "A people without a heritage are easily persuaded [controlled]." George Orwell added some intensity to this notion in his *1984* Inner Party motto, "He who controls the past, controls the future."

So let's take a look at our country's history, so we can better judge the current situation in our public schools. Since the very birth of the colonies in the 1600s until the mid-1900s, a Christian worldview was actually *encouraged* in all our schools, including public schools. For over 300 years of our nation's history, a Judeo-Christian worldview was widely acknowledged as the essential moral compass of our nation. There are literally thousands of primary quotes by Founders of the nation, such as Noah Webster, that demonstrate this. If you were a Christian parent of a public school student in those years, the prevailing winds would most often have been with you. School began with prayer, teachers integrated the Bible into daily lessons, and the Ten Commandments

---

[3] Thomas Jefferson, *Securing the Republic*, 1784

hung on most classroom walls. It has only been in the latter half of the twentieth century that a secular worldview has infiltrated and radically changed our schools. Of course not all schools espouse this worldview. We need to realize, however, that there has been a major shift towards the secularization of our educational system, and this radical change in worldview affects every student in public schools.

Where did the idea of public schools come from, anyway? The public schools in our nation actually originated with the founding Christians. Reading was so highly valued by the Puritans and most Protestant Reformers that they sought to make books available to and literacy a priority for every citizen. Up to that point in human history, education had generally been reserved for the upper classes, and primarily only for their sons. But the Puritan settlers believed that it was critical for everyone to know how to read the Bible, so that all citizens would be able to evaluate for themselves if the government was passing laws in accordance with Scripture. Psalm 119:160 (ESV) says, "The sum of your word is truth. And every one of your righteous rules endures forever." The Puritans understood this to mean that the only way to keep from being deceived or led astray was to know the Bible. They felt so strongly that every single person should be able to read the Bible that they started schools for everyone. One of the very first laws passed in their colonies was the "Old Deluder Satan Law" in Massachusetts in 1642, and Connecticut in 1647.

> It being one chief project of that old deluder, Satan, to keep men from the knowledge of the Scriptures, as in former time . . . It is therefore ordered . . . [that] after the Lord hath increased [the settlement] to the number of fifty households, [they] shall then forthwith appoint one within their town, to teach all such children as shall resort to him, to write and read . . . where any town shall increase to the number of one hundred families or households, they shall set up a grammar school.

Because the Christian worldview held that all mankind is created in the image of God, everyone was required to learn how to read, not just boys. The value that early American Christian settlers placed on reading the Bible radically changed the state of education. Literacy rates skyrocketed in our young nation to levels that the world had never before seen. By the time of the American Revolution in 1776, the literacy rate was over 90%.[4] Because the Puritans applied a Biblical worldview to education, America had the highest literacy rates in the history of the world.

One effect of the "Old Deluder Satan Law" that continued throughout the founding era of our nation was an emphasis on teaching Christian morality in public schools. This is clear in laws such as the Northwest Ordinance, which was signed into law by President Washington in 1789. It regulated how new states entering the Union were to value education and what was to be taught: "Religion, morality, and knowledge, being necessary to good government and the happiness of mankind, schools and the means of education shall forever be encouraged." This quote makes it clear that it was expected that every state's public schools would teach students about religion and morality, in addition to other subject matter. It is telling that the Northwest Ordinance was signed into law at the same time that the Founders were deciding on the wording of the First Amendment. Clearly, in the eyes of those politicians and Constitutional experts, the First Amendment did not in any way mean that Christian morality should be barred from schools (as many people today surmise).

It is important to note that many of the primary source quotes included in this book contain the word *religion*. Currently the word *religion* is used to mean simply any set of beliefs that is of supreme importance to someone. Therefore, several of our federal courts have correctly identified atheism, or secular humanism, as a religion, because it is also a system of such beliefs. But what did *religion* mean in the context of these quotes? Let's look at how Noah Webster's 1828 dictionary defines *religion*: "Includes a belief in the being and perfections of God, in the revelation of His will to man, in man's obligation to obey His commands, in a state of reward and punishment, and in man's accountableness to God; and also true godliness or piety of life, with the practice of all moral duties." Clearly the word *religion* in documents from the Founding era refers to a Christian worldview. We must keep this definition in mind when reading quotes from that time period.

---

[4] Kenneth Lockridge, *Literacy in Colonial New England*, University of Montana, 1974

What was the most widely used textbook in early U.S. schools? Many people today would be surprised to find out that it was the Bible. In fact, Fisher Ames, a signer of the Declaration of Independence, said this in 1801:

> [Why] should not the Bible regain the place it once held as a school book? Its morals are pure, its examples captivating and noble. The reverence for the Sacred Book that is thus early impressed lasts long.

Mr. Ames was noting that, at the turn of the century, some other textbooks, in addition to the Bible, were gaining popularity in schools. His declaration emphasizes his belief that the Bible should retain its place as a key teaching tool in schools. In a stroke of irony, it turns out that Fisher Ames is also the primary author of the "Establishment Clause" in the First Amendment of the Bill of Rights, which has now been misinterpreted by many people to mean the total "separation of church and state." (We will discuss the Establishment Clause and its misinterpretation later.)

The second most widely used textbook for the first two hundred years of our nation's history was a book called *The New England Primer*. Nearly every Founder of our nation learned to read by using this book, including the writers of the Declaration of Independence, the Constitution, and the Bill of Rights. More than six million of these books were printed and sold from the late 1600s to the early 1900s (a phenomenal number in those days, before efficient modern printing presses). Let's see what was included in this book that was taught to all 1st graders.

To learn the alphabet, students were shown the letter, along with a picture and a rhyming scheme. Here is the text for A—C.

A—In Adams fall, we sinned all.
B—Heaven to find, the Bible mind.
C—Christ crucified, for sinners died.[5]

Students also memorized the Lord's Prayer ("Our Father, which art in Heaven, hallowed be thy name. Thy kingdom come. Thy will be done . . . "), as well as a short *catechism*, which was a list of 107 questions and answers defining core Christian beliefs.

---

[5] *The New-England Primer*, Boston, 1777

Almost every lesson in this textbook was focused on Christianity and the importance of living according to a Biblical worldview! Bear in mind that these lessons were being taught in all public schools throughout our nation. I encourage everyone to read *The New England Primer*. Because of that little textbook, virtually every graduate of a public school in the Founders' era would have had a more comprehensive Biblical worldview than many seminary students of today. A 1900 reprint of the New England Primer said this book has "contributed, perhaps more than any other book except the Bible, to the molding of those sturdy generations that gave to America its liberty and its institutions."

When some Delaware Native American chiefs asked that their youth be educated in our United States public schools, George Washington replied, "You do well to wish to learn our arts and ways of life, and above all, the religion of Jesus Christ . . . Congress will do everything they can to assist you in this wise intention."[6]

So we see that—until very recently—Christianity was at the foundation of our American educational system. The censoring of Christianity from our American educational system is a very recent— and even a bizarre—phenomenon. (See Chapter 5 for more details.)

Today's Worldview Gale

There is a lot of talk these days about competing, or battling, *worldviews*. What is a worldview, anyway? One dictionary defines *worldview* as "a comprehensive concept of the world." People's worldviews influence how they interact with the world around them. It is the "lens" through which they view the world, influencing what they say, believe, think, and do. It explains why similar people with similar backgrounds can respond very differently to the same situation.

There are many different worldviews, and everyone ascribes to one of them, or at least incorporates one as their predominant way of influencing how they interact with the world. For the purposes of this book, we will simplify the discussion and look

6 George Washington, "Speech to the Delaware Indian Chiefs," 1779; published in *The Writings of George Washington*, 1932

primarily at two worldviews in direct conflict within our culture today: a Biblical worldview and a secular humanist worldview.

Biblical Worldview
- Theistic, one God revealed in three persons (Father, Son, Holy Spirit)
- Spiritual realm that is unseen, in addition to the seen physical universe
- God is Creator of everything
- Absolute moral truth

Secular Humanist Worldview
- Atheistic religion
- Naturalist, there is no spiritual realm
- Life arose randomly through materialistic Darwinian evolution
- Moral relativism

Obviously, these two worldviews clash quite dramatically. The secular humanist views the world from a naturalistic perspective. In other words, "what you see is what you get." There is nothing else out there in the universe but what we can see and feel. In contrast, the Biblical worldview maintains that there is a spiritual realm as well as a physical one. For the secular humanist, the universe, planets, chemicals, and all life arose randomly through evolution, as opposed to being created by God. A secular humanist believes in moral relativism, which means that what is true for one person is not necessarily true for someone else. Not only would this mean that moral truth varies from person to person, but also what is moral in one period and time is not necessarily moral in another. Simply put, the secular humanist believes that morals can evolve over time. What is morally true for one generation might change for the next generation.

The Founders of our nation for the most part operated from, and promoted, a Christian worldview. Fast forward to our current situation. In most areas of public education, the worldview battle for Christians as it would be understood by Fisher Ames has been all but lost. That is to say, many of the Founders of our nation, who advocated for the Bible being used as a moral foundation for public education, would look at our schools in utter dismay. Men like Fisher Ames and Noah Webster actually desired for the Bible and a Christian worldview to be presented and valued in public schools. They believed American citizens should have the freedom to practice any religion of choice (i.e., they did not advocate for a state-mandated religion), but they unashamedly acknowledged Christianity as the moral foundation of our nation, especially in schools. That particular battle has been generally lost.

A secular worldview gained momentum in the middle of the twentieth century and rapidly influenced the educational system. Famous educator and secular humanist John Dewey (considered the father of our modern educational system) in 1933 captured the secular agenda in the following quote:

> Faith in the prayer-hearing God is an unproved and outmoded faith. There is no God and there is no soul. Hence, there are no needs for the props of traditional religion. With dogma and creed excluded, then immutable truth is dead and buried. There is no room for fixed, natural law or moral absolutes.[7]

Dewey was also a chief signer of the Humanist Manifesto in 1933, which states: "Religious humanists regard the universe as self-existing and not created. Humanism believes that man is a part of nature and that he has emerged as a result of a continuous process." In other words, man was not created, but has evolved. John Dewey believed in Marxist ideals and set out to transform our educational system from one that was decentralized and encouraged Christian morality to one that was centralized or government-controlled, in line with his socialist ideals. He also wanted to remove any reliance on Christian morality from the educational system.[8]

Dewey was part of a movement that at the time was heavily influenced by Marxist thinking. Karl Marx's philosophy birthed the communist movement. Marx believed that communism would result in a utopia for mankind. In a communist society, citizens work for the government and the government in turn is supposed to meet all their needs. The system is similar to a parent taking care of their children, while the children have no authority.

---

[7] John Dewey, "Soul Searching," Teacher Magazine, September 1933
[8] David Breese, *7 Men Who Rule the World from the Grave*, Moody Press, 1990

In theory, the system is supposed to result in a perfect distribution of goods and services to all those in need.

History reveals a dreadfully different reality. One of Marx's key assumptions is flawed. The communist and socialist ideologies, based on Marx's flawed view, assume that mankind is inherently good. Yet Christians know that humans have an inherent sinful nature. We know that without Christ, mankind tends towards evil and selfishness rather than selflessness. It is only by the infilling of the Holy Spirit that we can truly be good.

Communist governments are atheistic in nature, and the State or Party is, in effect, worshiped as the supreme and all-powerful deity. So what will happen if all power in a country is held by a behemoth of a communist government, a government composed of people who believe themselves to be the supreme authority (God) in the world? The sinful human beings who make up the behemoth will hold the power of life and death over everyone else, they will oppressively abuse this power, and it will be almost impossible to remove the power from their hands. Hence the tragedies we see in countries that have had the terrible misfortune to be ruled by a Communist, or Marxist, regime. At least 170 million people were killed by atheistic governments in the twentieth century alone. In Communist China, over 70 million were murdered under the rule of Mao Tse Tung. Lenin, Stalin, and Soviet Communists killed over 50 million people.[9] The famous Russian writer Dostoyevsky, a Christian, was indeed accurate when he asserted that, "If God is dead, then all things are possible!"[10]

Communism and socialism assume that governments can handle all spheres of life more efficiently and more equitably than families, free markets, or the Church. Who needs God when you have the government? Dewey and his cohorts believed in Marxist ideals, therefore he brought these ideals into his teaching and reform of the educational system in America. Much of Dewey's philosophy focuses on self-actualization and the "socialization" of the child. He wrote frequently about the schools generating a child able to contribute to the social order of society. However, his philosophy is always devoid of religious principles. Dewey hated

---

[9] R.J. Rummel, *Death by Government*, Transaction Publishers, 2007
[10] Fyodor Dostoyevsky, *The Brothers Karamazov*, 1880

religion, especially the concept of absolute moral truth. His is just one example of how a secular humanist worldview has been integrated into our modern public educational system.[11]

A strong partnership between humanists and public education developed in the twentieth century. Charles Potter points out in his book *Humanism: A New Religion*, "Education is thus a most powerful ally of humanism, and every American school is a school of humanism. What can a theistic Sunday school's meeting for an hour once a week and teaching only a fraction of the children do to stem the tide of the five-day program of humanistic teaching?"[12]

A secular worldview has now secured its place as the default worldview in our educational system. Warren Nord, retired Director of the Humanities Program at the University of North Carolina, said this in his book *Religion & American Education*: "Much secular education nurtures a 'passive' hostility towards religion . . . public schooling clearly and forcefully discourages students from thinking about the world in religious ways."[13]

Perhaps the most influential educator is one who teaches the teachers. Richard Rorty, prominent twentieth century philosopher, said this in a disturbing quote:

> [I], like most Americans who teach humanities or social science in colleges and universities . . . try to arrange things so that students who enter as bigoted, homophobic, religious fundamentalists will leave college with views more like our own . . . The fundamentalist parents of our fundamentalist students think that the entire "American liberal establishment" is engaged in a conspiracy. The parents have a point . . .
>
> We are going to go right on trying to discredit you in the eyes of your children, trying to strip your fundamentalist religious community of dignity, trying to make your views seem silly rather than discussable. We are not so inclusivist as to tolerate intolerance such as yours . . . I think those students are lucky to find themselves under the benevolent Herrschaft [domination] of people like me, and to have escaped the grip of their frightening, vicious, dangerous parents.[14]

[11] David Breese, *7 Men Who Rule the World from the Grave*, Moody Press, 1990

[12] Charles Potter, *Humanism: A New Religion*, New York: Simon and Schuster, 1930

[13] Warren Nord, *Religion & American Education*, UNC Press, 1995

[14] Richard Rorty, *Rorty and His Critics*, Blackwell Publishers, 2000, p. 21-22

There is a strong liberal, secular humanist influence among the professors who are in charge of training educators. One of the most astounding and almost unbelievable examples of such academics is Bill Ayers. Both Ayers and his wife, Bernadine Dohrn, were involved in anti-government terrorist activities in the 1960s and were involved in the international Communist movement's "terrorist fifth column" within the United States.[15] Ayers was a top leader in the Weather Underground, which he describes as "an American Red Army." He admitted to bombing the Pentagon, among other targets:

> Everything was absolutely ideal on the day I bombed the Pentagon. The sky was blue. The birds were singing. And the b*****ds were finally going to get what was coming to them . . . Guilty as h***. Free as a bird. America is a great country.[16]

After their terrorist involvement, both Ayers and Dohrn became "respected" academics. Ayers was a "Distinguished" Professor of Education at the University of Illinois-Chicago, active at influencing teachers, and Dohrn taught law at Northwestern University. Both are unrepentant about their terrorist activities. Can you imagine if the Oklahoma City bomber became a teacher of teachers? Yet because of Ayers liberal academic bent and positioning, not many people express discomfort about his role as an influential academic figure. The fact that the mainstream news media has not focused more attention on Ayers is revealing. It would make an intriguing story: "Unrepentant, self-professed Communist terrorist now responsible for helping train the teachers of tomorrow." Although Ayers has been covered on more conservative news programs, there has been little in the mainstream media. When I give talks and mention Bill Ayers, few people have even heard of him. Following the 9/11 attacks, David Horowitz, founder of the Center for the Study of Popular Culture and a former Marxist himself, had this to say: "Many of us have children in secondary schools who, in this hour of mourning, have been lectured by their teachers on America's sins and

---

[15] http://www.thenewamerican.com/usnews/crime/item/15228-respectable-terrorists

[16] Bill Ayers, *Fugitive Days: A Memoir*, 2001

chickens coming home to roost. The political friends of Bill Ayers and Bernadine Dohrn have been busily at work for the last two decades seeding our educational culture with anti-American poisons that could one day destroy us."[17]

Most Christians nowadays either do not know that a worldview battle even took place, or do not really understand the history of the battle or how it was lost. Though some Christians are still taking up legal and intellectual arms in an attempt to have the Bible included in our public school curricula, I believe there is slim chance that a Christian worldview will ever be as esteemed as it once was in our public educational system. We have transitioned from primarily protecting the Bible in public schools to protecting *students* from rampant hostility against a Christian worldview.

One key to protecting students from the worldview gale that blows through most public school classrooms is to simply become educated about the trends and our rights in the public arena. We need to understand the prevailing winds so they do not throw our families off course. This is why it is so crucial for parents to be as involved as possible in their children's schooling. When parents take time to volunteer in the classroom, skim textbooks and homework assignments, and pray with other Christians at school, they gain insight into the trends at their school. They will also have a better chance of dealing with important issues that may affect their kids *before* these issues arise. This book will serve parents as they prepare for the worldview gales.

My Journey through the Worldview Gale

I did not realize, when the atheist parent complained about my 5th-grade class discussion about the Pledge of Allegiance, that the weather had truly changed in my classroom. I had entered stormy seas without much thought. About a month later, while discussing Columbus's voyage, another inquisitive hand was raised. We had been having a brief discussion about the motives for Columbus's explorations. The textbook focused almost entirely on wealth and power and left out nearly all mention of Columbus's complex yet

---

[17] David Horowitz, "Allies in War," FrontPageMagazine.com, Sept 17, 2001

serious ambitions to spread Christianity. I explained briefly about his aims. A hand popped up. *What does it mean to be a Christian?* Pause. I took about fifteen seconds to explain that a Christian is someone who follows the teachings of Jesus Christ. I thought that Christianity played an important enough role in world and U.S. history to define the term.

Like clockwork, my principal once again paid me a visit shortly after class. Visibly irritated, she asked, "What are you doing talking about Jesus Christ in class?" I relayed the discussion about Columbus. After my explanation, she agreed that it was reasonable to answer the student's question about Christianity. I told my principal that I would be happy to meet with any concerned parent and have an open discussion about what I taught and why. I explained that it is very difficult to resolve issues with an anonymous person. My principal was firm; the parent wanted to remain anonymous.

During my commute home, I processed the emerging pattern. It was clear this parent was ready to complain at any opportunity if God, Jesus, or Christianity came up in the classroom. I reflected on the amazing efficiency and tenacity of this anonymous parent. The child, under the parent's prompting, must have been attentively waiting for any mention of God, Jesus, or Christianity. If the topic arose, which it rarely did, the child would go home and inform the parent. The parent would then immediately call the principal and obviously grossly exaggerate what was said. The principal would drop everything and start the walk over to my class. I realized that I had two choices. It was early in the year and I was facing a 5th-grade curriculum that included studying the Puritans, the Mayflower Compact, and reading prominent Christian author C. S. Lewis's novel, *The Lion, the Witch and the Wardrobe.* I could either tip-toe around Christianity and cower in the face of disgruntled anonymity, or I could simply teach an accurate account of the role of Christianity in history, literature, and current events as the topic surfaced naturally in the curriculum. Quite honestly, if it had been the previous school year, I probably would have cowered. However, it happened that a Christian teacher at another school had recently shared some material with me that outlined information on a teacher's rights in the classroom.

I decided not to intentionally avoid Christianity and to stand firm with what I knew was appropriate for the curriculum.

I didn't have a chance to test my newfound courage for several months. Winter came and went. Another conflict arose in early spring. I had overviewed the major holidays from around the world throughout the year: Ramadan, Diwali, Kwanzaa, Hanukkah, and Chinese New Year (which actually is a religious holiday), among others. When Easter came around, I thought it would be reasonable to do a lesson on this holiday, as I had covered so many others. When I presented the lesson to my principal, she became visibly annoyed and said that she would check with the district office. Her ultimate response was, "No way." I found this very ironic, coming from a district that prided itself on diversity and tolerance and that explored other religions openly. I had just been encouraged by the school district to attend an all-day training on the Hindu religion. Another Cupertino middle school had organized a "living history month" around the Islamic holiday of Ramadan. Throughout each school day the students pretended to be Muslims, which included bringing their prayer carpets wherever they went, praying five times a day toward the east, memorizing the Five Pillars of Islam, learning about Mohammed's life and death, and memorizing parts of the Koran and Hadith. But apparently Christianity was different, as my principal expressed in an email:

> Easter and Christianity should not be part of your classroom instruction or discussions. The subjects are not part of 5th-grade standards and curriculum. I also feel that you are being insensitive to our diverse religious community . . .

I honored my principal's request, but I found her response terribly inconsistent, given that so many other religious holidays had been studied in our class and at our school. It was also puzzling from an educational standpoint because the study of Christianity is an important part of the California Content Standards for 5th grade. While Christianity was a legitimate subject according to the Content Standards, as soon as even a mention of it arose, the principal shut down the conversation. Each state is responsible for clearly defining what is to be taught at each grade level. These curriculum requirements are known as Content Standards. The table below shows several obvious areas of the 5th-grade curriculum that dealt directly with Christianity.

From the California "History Social Studies Framework and Content Standards (2001 edition)" for 5th Grade

General Concept	Quote from Content Standards Document
Judeo-Christian foundations of the nation	"This course focuses on one of the most remarkable stories in history: the creation of a new nation founded on Judeo-Christian religious thinking." (p.64)
Explorers	"In this unit students will concentrate on European explorers who sought trade routes, economic gain, adventure, national glory, and 'the greater glory of God.'" (p.64)
Pilgrims	"The Pilgrims' religious beliefs and their persecution by the Church of England should be fully discussed." (p.65)
Religious life of colonies	"Students should learn about the political, religious, economic, and social life of the colonies." (p.66)
Puritans	"The story of the Puritans is equally important in light of their enduring influence on American literature, education, and attitudes toward life and work. Inspired by their religious zeal, Puritans sought to establish a new Zion, "a city on a hill," where they might live out their religious ideals." [Jesus coined the term "city on a hill" in Matt. 5:14] (p.66)
Religious life of colonies	"Describe the religious aspects of the earliest colonies (e.g., Puritanism in Massachusetts, Anglicanism in Virginia, Catholicism in Maryland, Quakerism in Pennsylvania)." (p.72)
First Great Awakening	"Identify the significance and leaders of the First Great Awakening, which marked the shift in religious ideas, practices, and allegiances in the colonial period, the growth of religious toleration, and free exercise of religion." (p.72)

The Standards were clear that Christianity was woven throughout various historical topics that I was required to be teaching in the classroom. However, it was becoming clear that the administration believed that the "separation of church and state" only applied to Christianity, but not to other religions. It was clear that I was experiencing religious censorship and that I might need to get some legal help in resolving the issue. I started to do some research into organizations that could help me work with the school district in educating them on the appropriate inclusion of religion in the curriculum. I contacted Alliance Defending Freedom (ADF) and they simply asked me to keep records of all correspondence with the administration. There was not much to keep track of initially because the number of times that God, Jesus, or Christianity came up were very infrequent. The vast majority of my curricula were very secular in nature.

The next complaint by the anonymous parent arose when I did a ten-minute lesson on the National Day of Prayer. For three previous years I had taught the same patriotic lesson, with quotes from George Washington and Abraham Lincoln. I had never had any complaints from any student or parent. The lesson focused on the historic role that prayer played in our nation's founding. I did not talk about the value of prayer or even hint that prayer was something that the students should do. I did not mention that I pray. I concluded by reading part of the then-current president's official proclamation on the most recent National Day of Prayer. It was after this lesson that a parent wrote me an email expressing that it was not appropriate to even mention the National Day of Prayer in public schools, because of the infamous "separation of church and state." In an anonymous email sent via the principal, the parent said this: "Given the historic separation between church and state, this kind of material seems to run counter to the tradition of public school education in America."

This would be a good time to recall that our national motto is actually, "In God We Trust." The word "God" is in our motto, in the Pledge of Allegiance, and on our money. Congress prays. Our presidents are sworn into office using a Bible and with prayer. Certainly, the president of our country should not be banned from public schools because he mentions God, Christianity, or the Bible. However, this particular parent would not tolerate any mention of

God whatsoever. Without even talking about the lesson with me, my principal emailed me and said that she was in agreement with the parent, stating:

> I agree with the parent and am, hereby, directing you to stop sending out materials of a religious nature with your students. I am directing you to provide me with an "advance" copy of materials you will be sending home at least two days prior to their being sent out so I can make sure that the materials will not be of concern to the parents or violate the separation of religion and public education.

Separation of religion and public education? I was astonished at this statement, as she knew there were numerous places in public education curriculum that explored various religions and it was even mandated in our Content Standards. Surely she should have known that a complete separation of religion and public education would leave students with a hole in their education. Even our federal courts have realized this fact, as reflected in the ruling below:

> The First Amendment was never intended to insulate our public institutions from any mention of God, the Bible or religion. When such insulation occurs, another religion, such as secular humanism, is effectively established.[18]

Having been silenced by the principal, I carried on with teaching my class, choosing lessons based on our state curriculum standards. Little did I know that just around the corner was the straw that would break the teacher's back. For a lesson on the Declaration of Independence, I wanted to hand out several primary source documents from our nation's history. Some of these documents had Christian references, such as William Penn's *Frame of Government* and Samuel Adams's *The Rights of the Colonists*.

I wasn't going to use any documents with added opinions or analysis—simply primary source documents written by the Founding Fathers themselves. After I submitted my lesson, the principal denied my request. In effect, the principal said it was fine for the students to learn *about* William Penn and the founding of Pennsylvania, but only through textbook paraphrases. I was not

---

[18] United States Federal District Court, in *Crockett v. Sorenson* (1983)

allowed to hand out the actual document itself, she said, because Penn's document violated the "separation of church and state." When he described the purpose of government in this foundational document in U.S. history, you see, William Penn had the "audacity" to quote the Bible.

> When the great and wise *God* had made the world, of all his creatures it pleased him to choose man his deputy to rule it; and to fit him for so great a charge and trust, he did not only qualify him with skill and power but with integrity to use them justly . . . but this is not all, he opens and carries the matter of government a little further: "Let every soul be subject to the higher powers; for there is no power but of *God.* The powers that be are ordained of *God:* whosoever therefore resisteth the power, resisteth the ordinance of *God.* For rulers are not a terror to good works, but to evil: wilt thou then not be afraid of the power? Do that which is good, and thou shalt have praise of the same. He is the minister of God to thee for good. Wherefore ye must needs be subject, not only for wrath, but for conscience' sake." [Penn quoting from Romans 13:1–3]
>
> This settles the divine right of government beyond exception, and that for two ends: first, to terrify evildoers; secondly, to cherish those that do well; which gives government a life beyond corruption and makes it as durable in the world, as good men shall be. So that government seems to me a part of religion itself, a thing sacred in its institution and end.[19]

Yet our school textbook did not quote anything from the document itself (more on historical revisionism later), but merely summed up Penn's intentions by stating, "Penn hoped to establish a colony where Quakers could practice their religion in freedom . . . Penn planned for Pennsylvania to be a place of peace where people would treat each other fairly."[20] The textbook summarized the document by commenting, "A written plan for government that granted religious freedom to colonists in Pennsylvania."[21] It mentioned nothing about God, Scripture, or the source of Penn's purpose of government rooted in a Biblical worldview. This helps us understand why primary sources should be included in teach-

---

[19] William Penn, *Frame of Government of the Province of Pennsylvania*, 1682

[20] 5th Grade Social Studies Textbook, *United States*, McGraw-Hill, 1999, p. 211

[21] 5th Grade Social Studies Textbook, *A New Nation*, McGraw-Hill, 2000, p. 323

ing at all grade levels. In fact, the California Framework Standards include an eloquent argument for using primary sources to help bring history to life:

> Teachers of history at all grade levels have recently begun to encourage their students not just to study history but to investigate it . . . Fundamental to this process are primary sources, which lie as much at the heart of history as experiments lie at the heart of science. Students of history should be given opportunities to read and analyze primary sources, to wrestle with their meanings, and to attempt to interpret them and place them in context.[22]

Although I shared this information with the principal, she still refused to allow me to include William Penn's *Frame of Government*, Samuel Adams's *The Rights of the Colonists*, and the first two paragraphs and last paragraph of the Declaration of Independence.

I made my case again in an email to my principal about why I wanted to include these three primary source documents in the lesson plan. I explained to her that my students were confused about where a citizen's rights came from in our fledgling country, this new form of government called a *constitutional republic*. The Declaration proclaims that their rights came directly from God; this was a revolutionary new concept in human history. The Declaration of Independence also states clearly that our country was founded on the principle that all American citizens—in fact everyone in the entire world—gets their rights from God, and that the role of all governments is to protect those God-given rights.

> We hold these truths to be self-evident, that all men are created equal, that they are endowed by their Creator with certain unalienable Rights, that among these are Life, Liberty and the pursuit of Happiness. — That to secure these rights, Governments are instituted among Men, deriving their just powers from the consent of the governed.

This short but incredibly foundational concept from the Declaration is what made the United States unique from all other

---

[22] *History–Social Science Framework for California Public Schools*, 2001 Edition with Content Standards, Appendix F, "Using Primary Sources in the Study of History"

governments in recorded history to that point. This concept was also woven throughout the various colonial governments leading up to the formation of the United States. But because my students were confused about the Founders' view of citizens' rights, I thought giving them access to certain key documents would help them better understand the concepts.

The email response from my principal—after I gave her these three primary source documents—read as follows:

> The materials you submitted yesterday are once again of a religious nature and are not appropriate to be used with your fifth grade students because the district honors separation of church and state in school. This is a repetition of what I told you in person and in my May 11th memo. You have a text book and adequate district resource materials to address the social studies standards. Since you are having difficulty, I suggest that you meet with the other three fifth grade teachers or I can find someone from the Department of Instruction to assist you . . . Please submit your weekly lesson plans to me for the remainder of the year so that I can better monitor your instruction in this area.

Some of the most important documents of our nation's founding were now deemed "of a religious nature." William Penn's *Frame of Government* and *The Rights of the Colonists* have been cited as some of the instrumental documents in shaping key ideas in our Declaration and form of government. However, my students were not allowed to even read them, "because the district honors separation of church and state in school." My principal also wanted to see all of my lesson plans, so she could make sure that any material remotely Christian would be censored from my class.

Even so, I was still very careful in what I taught in the classroom. As a Christian, I had a Biblical conviction to be strictly upright and honest with my choice in lesson plans. If it was not in the standards then I did not want to introduce it into the curriculum. As a public school teacher, I wanted to honor my contract of not using my classroom to proselytize my students. I simply wanted to teach history accurately. But the principal and school district would not allow it based on a false understanding of the separation of church and state. That student's first question which elicited the anonymous complaint, about why we say "under God" in the pledge, turned out to be a very important question indeed; it was one which the students were never able to understand, simply because I was prevented from showing them the primary source materials of our nation's founding. After much prayer and counsel, I filed a complaint within the federal courts the following year with the help of Alliance Defending Freedom. The goal of the case was to allow primary source documents with Christian references to be deemed an appropriate part of history curricula in public schools. The rest of my story regarding this court case is woven throughout this book.

Let's face it. Being an evangelical Christian is not very popular these days. Jesus warns us in the Bible that we should not seek popularity. Yet it is often really difficult for kids to withstand the pressures they face in school. It is important for parents, teachers and youth workers to understand how strong the prevailing winds of today feel to kids. We need to communicate with our kids about the issues they are facing. Regardless of your involvement with public schools—student, parent, staff, youth pastor, volunteer—it is crucial for you to be aware of which way the winds are blowing. There are a lot of resources to help you do this, and opportunities for you to connect with other Christians throughout this process, which we will discuss in later chapters. However, if we simply set sail and do not take the time to understand prevailing trends, we will be unprepared and continually tossed about by gale after gale, losing our course in one of the most important journeys of our lives.

CHAPTER 3

WHO IS YOUR FAMILY'S ANCHOR?

> We have this as a sure and steadfast anchor of the soul, a hope that enters into the inner place behind the curtain, where Jesus has gone as a forerunner on our behalf.
>
> —Hebrews 6:19–20

Several massive ship anchors decorated the grounds of my college campus. I (Sarah) remember running my fingers along the steel and imagining how many times they had been lowered into the stormy waters of Lake Michigan. I was awed by the weight of them. The anchor is crucial to navigation, preventing a ship from drifting off course in stormy seas, dangerous currents, or strong winds. Either by hooking into the bed of the sea or just by sheer mass, the anchor has holding power. Some anchors are as enormous as trucks, weighing thousands of pounds and heavy enough to make a tossing vessel stay put in raging weather. Raising children, especially in our increasingly secular culture, can also get stormy at times. But God is right there with us. He promises to be our anchor.

THE JOURNEY BEGINS WITH YOU

When I embarked on the adventure of marriage and parenting, I read books about these new people in my life who were now my family. How could I have a thriving marriage? How could I raise godly children? How could I grow into my new roles? I began to realize that if I wanted to be a great wife and mother, I needed to make my one true anchor, God, my number one priority in life. I learned that God wanted me to start with me—not my husband, not my children—and that meant me starting with Him.

In Hebrews 6:19, the author identifies hope in Christ as the "anchor of the soul." In this stormy life, we all need an anchor sometimes, don't we? Being weak and imperfect, we so easily drift into thought patterns or actions (or inactions) that are out of alignment with Biblical teachings. Or we might get caught in an emotional storm of wrong thinking, and pretty soon we are carried away by dangerous currents and find ourselves rationalizing our behavior. Days become weeks, weeks become years, until suddenly we realize that our personal walk with the Lord, and maybe even our faith and our family's faith, is far off course. The Bible calls us to be strongly anchored to Christ because He is the only One who can truly anchor us. Jesus is "the Way, the Truth, and the Life." Jesus is the One who keeps us safe in the storm. When we are anchored to Christ, our eyes are fixed on Him and our lives honor Him.

So how can we remain close to the "anchor of our soul?" The answers are relatively simple in print, yet only possible when we continually ask the Holy Spirit to empower us. The Bible urges us to draw close, pray, cry out, and petition Him. It pleads with us to stay in the Word and to fix our eyes on Jesus.

The truth is that *our faith life greatly influences our children.* This may feel convicting, but we often need a solid dose of conviction. A sociologist from the University of Notre Dame, Dr. Christian Smith, summarized the current research this way: "Most teenagers and their parents may not realize it, but a lot of research in the sociology of religion suggests that the most important social influence in shaping young people's religious lives is the religious life modeled and taught to them by their parents."[1] Kara Powell and Chap Clark state it this way in their book *Sticky Faith*: "More than even your support, it's who you are that shapes your kid. In fact, it's challenging to point to a Sticky Faith factor that is more significant than you. How you express and live out your faith may have a greater influence on your son or daughter than anything else . . . you

---

[1] Christian Smith with Melinda Lundquist Denton, *Soul Searching: The Religious and Spiritual Lives of American Teenagers*, Oxford Univ. Press, 2005, p.56

are an ongoing companion, guide and fellow journeyer."[2] Similar findings spring up in many spheres of life. Business statistics show that employees tend to do what their leaders do. As famous business leadership expert John C. Maxwell says, "A leader is one who knows the way, goes the way, and shows the way." If leaders are negative, employees will be negative. So if my desire is to help my children develop a vibrant and anchored Christian faith, then I need to pursue my faith with all my heart, mind, soul, and strength.

The Bible also warns us that we are in dangerous waters if we try to sail off alone, without encouragement and support from other Christians. Although our journey is personal, we also have a responsibility to involve others. We humans are imperfect, and we can expect many trials and disappointments along the way. Those disappointments should not be an excuse to quit on meaningful relationships with other Christians. The author of the book of Hebrews admonishes us to keep meeting together in the fellowship of other Christians. James says we ought to confess our sins to each other. Paul tells us to stand firm together, striving side by side in unity for the sake of the gospel of peace.

For our family, involvement with other Christians has been critical to our spiritual growth. Small discipleship/accountability groups have been the best tool to help Stephen and me actually *do* what the Bible says, not just read what it says. Of course we make mistakes, but the encouragement and prayer of other Christians helps us right the ship and get back on track. The international organization called Community Bible Study has helped me (Sarah) become a student of the Bible and has provided me great fellowship with other women. In short, your journey begins with you, but we need to involve other Christians as well. (We will discuss this important topic in greater detail in later chapters.)

GETTING YOUR SPOUSE ON BOARD

Your spouse may not always feel as much urgency about equipping your children to stand firm in the faith as you do. If this

---

[2] Kara Powell and Chap Clark, *Sticky Faith: Everyday Ideas to Build Lasting Faith in Your Kids*, Zondervan, 2011, p.24

is the case, it might be time for a heart-to-heart talk with them about the role that faith in Christ plays in your and your family's lives. Perhaps God is wanting to bring up the issue of life priorities and of creating a vision for your family. It might be useful to read together some chapters from books such as *You Lost Me* by David Kinnaman or *Sticky Faith* by Kara Powell and Chap Clark. These books talk about the reality of children leaving the faith; they force us to examine if we truly care if one of our own children were to leave the faith. It might be a good idea to sit down with your pastor and youth pastor and ask for their help in creating a family vision for passing on a love for, and commitment to, Christ. It would also be wise to discuss differences you and your spouse have in this area.

You can't choose your spouse's anchor for them. Many wives and husbands have spouses who are not Christian, who are not prioritizing their faith, or who have walked away from the faith. This is a tough situation and it will require you to persevere in prayer. Nagging your spouse will not help. If this is your story, then you will have to rely even more heavily on the Lord's guidance, as well as the resources in the body of Christ. Hopefully you have or can build a faith community at your church or home group that will gather around you. Pray for wisdom to create opportunities for your kids to grow in their faith.

BUILDING YOUR FAMILY'S WORLDVIEW AT HOME

Research shows clearly that a child's faith and worldview are mainly built at home, one building block at a time. Church, youth groups, conferences, and parachurch ministries can all provide wonderful and critical tools, but these tools are best used in concert with strong parental involvement. Research backs up Deuteronomy 6:5–9, which captures the heart of how to pass our faith on to the next generation:

> You shall love the LORD your God with all your heart and with all your soul and with all your might. And these words that I command you today shall be on your heart. You shall teach them diligently to your children, and shall talk of them when

you sit in your house, and when you walk by the way, and when you lie down, and when you rise. You shall bind them as a sign on your hand, and they shall be as frontlets between your eyes. You shall write them on the doorposts of your house and on your gates.

In essence, this passage tells us that what happens under your own roof, around the dinner table, in conversations, and at bedtime prayers, matters a lot. The Christian Research Institute (www.equip.org) says this:

Parents must embrace the fact that the home is where actual learning occurs and that *their* faith is essential for a successful handoff. Children don't want to just hear what mom and dad think about Christianity; they want to see that these beliefs make a difference in daily living within the context of a heart-level relationship. When a parent's faith is not lived out at all times, it is perceived as merely a hobby unrelated to reality. This inconsistency causes kids to compartmentalize their spiritual lives and eventually outgrow beliefs they have never seen modeled.

But let's be honest. In the competition for our time, there are a million things that often finish far ahead of faith and world-view-equipping. The effects of this time and worldview tug-of-war are reflected in the statistics—there is a worldview crisis among evangelical youth. Less than ten percent of Christian teens have even a basic Biblical worldview.[3] We must be very intentional in our equipping strategy, or passing on our faith and values to our children simply will not happen.

There are many ways we can help equip our families with a strong faith and worldview. From the time our children are young, we can train them up in the Christian faith. Making a family devotional or prayer time a priority can be a great tool. Our family has family devotionals, and each person gets to share what they've been learning in their personal quiet times. One family we know hosts an "apologetics and worldview night" at their home, for kids and their parents. They have dinner, watch a DVD together, and

---

[3] Barna Research Group, "Teens Evaluate the Church-Based Ministry They Received As Children," July 8, 2003

then discuss the material. For most people in our culture (including Christians), such a Friday night get-together might not have the same appeal as watching the latest superhero movie, but this family made it a priority and has stuck with it. They have made it even more fun by inviting other families, and they say that all the kids have been very engaged. Our church home group hosted an Alpha class, and many of the teens and tweens were involved. Not only did they learn the basics of the Christian faith, but they also were able to be involved in evangelism first-hand.

When you go to Christian events, try to take your children. For almost a decade, our ministry has organized an event called the Christian Youth Summit (www.ChristianYouthSummit.org), which draws hundreds of young people from across the Northwest. The mission of the Summit is to empower and equip teens with a solid Biblical worldview before they leave home. Although we also market the Summit to parents, we have been surprised at how difficult it is to get many parents to commit to attend. We are constantly having to convince parents how powerful it can be to dialogue with their kids. Our church culture has evolved into one that wants to farm out faith and worldview-equipping to the pastors and youth workers. Yet no one and nothing can replace a parent's role in praying for, encouraging, and equipping their children. The bonus is that as you shepherd and equip your children, your faith is enriched too. One mom who attended the Christian Youth Summit with her children said this about her experience, "Now, more than ever, I want my children to have as much information as possible to support their faith in God and His Word. And for the first time in my 46 years, I feel confident in defending my faith as well."

We need to start somewhere, even if we feel ill-equipped or fearful that we will face difficult questions from our children. As the saying goes, God can't steer a parked car (or in this case a ship). You may find the following organizations and curricula helpful in equipping your family to be students of the Word, with a Biblical worldview. There are many more out there, and as you journey, you will find more resources.

Organizations

- AWANA
- BIOLA University
- Community Bible Study
- Prepare the Way Ministries/Christian Youth Summit
- Sean McDowell Worldview Ministries
- Stand to Reason
- Summit Ministries

Curricula

- Alpha/The Alpha Course
- Gateways to Better Education's Keeping the Faith in Public Schools
- GodQuest
- God's Not Dead
- Prepare the Way Ministries' Standing Firm
- True U
- The Truth Project

Books

- *The Case for Christ* by Lee Strobel
- *The Case for Faith* by Lee Strobel
- *The Case for a Creator* by Lee Strobel
- *Total Truth* by Nancy Pearcy
- *More Than a Carpenter* by Josh and Sean McDowell
- *Evidence that Demands a Verdict* by Josh McDowell
- *The Unshakable Truth* by Josh and Sean McDowell
- *Questioning the Bible* by Jonathan Morrow
- *Five Sacred Crossings* by Craig Hazen
- *Love Your God with All Your Mind* by JP Moreland
- *Cold Case Christianity* by J. Warner Wallace
- *Keeping Your Kids on God's Side* by Natasha Crain
- *The Bible's Answers to 100 of Life's Biggest Questions* by Geisler & Jimenez

It's usually good to start the equipping process with the most common questions your children will face. The biggest question you will likely encounter in today's culture is, "Who is Jesus?" We have found in our interactions with young people that this question is often a great struggle for them. It is so prevalent to paint Jesus as simply a great moral teacher, just another prophet, or even a mythological figure. (These fallacious arguments are easily dealt with using extra-Biblical primary source documents; see Prepare the Way's curriculum, *Standing Firm*, for more information.) The question "Who is Jesus?" is the central question of the Christian faith; it is the defining question of our faith. C. S. Lewis said this in *Mere Christianity*:

> I am trying here to prevent anyone saying the really foolish thing that people often say about Him: I'm ready to accept Jesus as a great moral teacher, but I don't accept his claim to be God. That is the one thing we must not say. A man who was merely a man and said the sort of things Jesus said would not be a great moral teacher. He would either be a lunatic—on the level with the man who says he is a poached egg—or else he would be the Devil of Hell. You must make your choice. Either this man was, and is, the Son of God, or else a madman or something worse. You can shut him up for a fool, you can spit at him and kill him as a demon or you can fall at his feet and call him Lord and God, but let us not come with any patronising nonsense about his being a great human teacher. He has not left that open to us. He did not intend to. . . . Now it seems to me obvious that He was neither a lunatic nor a fiend: and consequently, however strange or terrifying or unlikely it may seem, I have to accept the view that He was and is God.[4]

Another major doubt that many young people have nowadays is about the reliability of the Bible, which is under great attack. Yet there are so many incredible resources out there that show that the Bible is the most reliable book in all of antiquity![5] These very logical arguments often collect dust on bookshelves, and many parents do not even know how to defend the reliability of the Bible. Because many students do not know the basic

---

[4] C. S. Lewis, *Mere Christianity*, 1952
[5] Josh McDowell, *The New Evidence That Demands a Verdict*, Nelson, 1999

arguments for the reliability of the Bible, their faith crumbles like a house of cards when even just one professor degrades the Bible.

In summary, it is critical to instill a comprehensive Biblical worldview in our children from an early age. However, while knowledge is important, it only goes so far.

THE POWER OF A LOVING RELATIONSHIP AND WITNESS

Ultimately, our journey to equip our family with a strong faith and worldview must be rooted in love and prayer. Paul so clearly captures this message in First Corinthians 13:

> If I speak in the tongues of men and of angels, but have not love, I am only a resounding gong or a clanging cymbal. If I have the gift of prophecy and can fathom all mysteries and all knowledge, and if I have a faith that can move mountains, but have not love, I am nothing. If I give all I possess to the poor and surrender my body to the flames, but have not love, I gain nothing. Love is patient, love is kind. It does not envy, it does not boast, it is not proud. It is not rude, it is not self-seeking, it is not easily angered, it keeps no record of wrongs. Love does not delight in evil but rejoices with the truth. It always protects, always trusts, always hopes, always perseveres. Love never fails.

We may use the best curricula in the world, read the Bible every day as a family, eat dinner together frequently, and attend all the best conferences, but if we are not rooted in love, we lack the most important key to encouraging our kids to be disciples of Christ. We must communicate through our words, actions, and time that we love our children and want the best for them. We always need to keep our family relationships as important priorities, praying *for* our children and *with* our children.

I have always been impacted by the incident in Numbers 20:9–13, where Moses was barred by God from entering the Promised Land. Instead of merely speaking to the rock (to make water flow from it) as God had commanded, Moses struck the rock twice and spoke harshly.

> So Moses took the staff from the Lord's presence, just as he commanded him. He and Aaron gathered the assembly together in

front of the rock and Moses said to them, "Listen, you rebels, must we bring you water out of this rock?" Then Moses raised his arm and struck the rock twice with his staff. Water gushed out, and the community and their livestock drank. But the Lord said to Moses and Aaron, "Because you did not trust in me enough to honor me as holy in the sight of the Israelites, you will not bring this community into the land I give them." These were the waters of Meribah, where the Israelites quarreled with the Lord and where he was proved holy among them.

Although there are several interpretations of why there were such drastic consequences for Moses, it has always rung true to me that it was because he did not represent God well to the Israelites. Moses was their spiritual leader. He was communicating on behalf of God, and was given the important mission to represent God and His character to the Israelites. Yet at a critical point in history, Moses gave in to the temptation to get angry. We must represent God well to our children, treating them with love and compassion, and not harshly. Their faith will likely depend on it.

We, too, are at a critical time in history. I don't think there has been an era where the world has such access to our children. Anti-Christian messages are about as difficult to keep out of our homes as air. Music, pop stars, advertisements, TV shows, and movies bombard our children . . . and all with the mission of capturing their hearts. If we don't capture the hearts of our children, someone else certainly will. The best way to capture their hearts is to make sure we have loving relationships with them, even in the most difficult and challenging times. If we are living out our faith, our children should be witnessing love in our homes. If we preach that God is love and if we have the Holy Spirit in us, then by God's grace everything we do should be rooted in love. With all the stresses of life, of course this is challenging, but we cannot give up. When we fail, we should ask our children's forgiveness. Through healthy accountability, we should fail less often and gradually rejoice in more victory.

As our children grow in the confidence that they are greatly loved by their parents and their Heavenly Father, they become more fertile soil for the Truth. They will not only see that Jesus is their parents' anchor, but through prayer and by God's grace, Jesus will also become the anchor of their souls.

CHAPTER 4

JOIN THE ARMADA: DON'T JOURNEY ALONE

And let us consider how we may spur one another on toward love and good deeds, not giving up meeting together, as some are in the habit of doing, but encouraging one another—and all the more as you see the Day approaching.

—Hebrews 10:24–25

We all need each other. God created us to be more effective when we have other people for support, accountability, and encouragement. We need community for a number of important reasons: to shepherd our own spiritual growth and accountability, to provide meaningful mentoring relationships for our children, to provide access to information from organizations that are experts in certain areas, and to band together to accomplish larger goals and pursue movements within the Church or culture.

According to various studies on church attendance and worldviews, there are an estimated sixty to seventy million Bible-believing, evangelical Christians in America.[1] About one out of every three people in the United States believe the Bible is the actual Word of God and is to be taken literally.[2] The Church in

---

[1] Barna Group, "Barna Survey Examines Changes in Worldview Among Christians over the Past 13 Years," March 9, 2009

[2] Gallup, "One-Third of Americans Believe the Bible Is Literally True," May 27, 2007

America is truly an armada, if we would only realize it and work together.

Getting equipped to navigate the public school system and raise faithful children is no small task, and it helps to join the armada. Thankfully, there is a plethora of ways we can join with other Christians in our journey.

Plug into the Local Church for Your Own Spiritual Growth

You may think that pursuing Christian community is important in theory, but how much do you actually live it out? If you ask most people, they are lacking deep relationships. Many Christians, intentionally or by default, stay on the surface. The problem with surface relationships is that life frequently gets deep. Superficial Christianity does not cut it when life gets hard. I realized early on in my Christian walk that it is difficult to stay faithful alone. God has designed us to be in relationship with other Christians. Perhaps that is why there are so many *one another* exhortations in the Bible, and so many memorable and quotable verses about relationships: *iron sharpens iron . . . a cord of three strands is not easily broken . . . do not cease meeting together.*[3] Half of the New Testament is made up of heartfelt letters written to brothers and sisters in Jesus, most of whom were navigating some pretty tough waters at the time. We are meant to relate, help, pray for, encourage, and disciple *one another*. If we are isolated, we are vulnerable to doubt, temptation, and a gradual drift towards lukewarm faith. As we discussed in the previous chapter, keeping Christ as our personal anchor is a powerful witness to our children. However, few people can live for Christ without the help and encouragement of Christian fellowship. Every solid church that is effectively growing usually has great groups to plug into. If they don't, start one.

---

[3] Joel Comiskey, *Biblical Foundations for the Cell-Based Church*, CCS Publishing, 2012

ENGAGE THE LOCAL CHURCH FOR
INTERGENERATIONAL RELATIONSHIPS AND MENTORS

A strong Christian network not only helps us in our personal walks (which in turn helps our children with theirs), but research has also found that your family's participation in a strong Christian community that promotes intergenerational relationships helps children stick with their faith. Although parents are the most important role models for their children, it is powerful to have other positive and loving adult role models in kids' lives as well.

Fuller Seminary's "College Transition Project" studied how various factors affected college students staying plugged into the Christian faith in college. Kara Powell and Chap Clark describe their quest to find a "silver bullet" in their book *Sticky Faith*: "We haven't found that silver bullet. While the study of Scripture, small groups, mentoring, retreats, justice work, and a host of other ministry activities are important, the reality is that kids' spiritual growth is far more complicated than just one silver bullet. The closest our research has come to that definitive silver bullet is this sticky finding: for high school and college students, there is a relationship between attendance at church-wide worship services and Sticky Faith." They go on to describe what they call a "sticky web of relationships." They suggest reversing the normal youth ministry rule and encourage a 5:1 ratio of adults to youth: "We're not talking about five Sunday school teachers or five small group leaders. We're also not talking about five adults to whom you outsource the spiritual, emotional, social, and intellectual development of your kids. We're talking about five solid Christian adults whom you recruit to invest in your child in little, medium and big ways."

In response to a study done on why youth are leaving church, the Vice President of LifeWay Research stressed this point: "Church leaders should passionately and consistently challenge church members to maximize their influence with youth and young adults. Frequent and intentional contact can either prevent or counteract the tendency of some to drop out of church."[4] The point is, we may need to radically re-think what we mean by

---

[1] Brad Wagonner, http://www.lifeway.com/Article/LifeWay-Research-finds -reasons-18-to-22-year-olds-drop-out-of-church/

church. To many adults I interact with, church is where we go and socialize and listen to a good sermon. After church, the conversation is often about how good (or not) the sermon was. It can become very self-focused and self-serving and we can easily see why the American church is often called "consumer-oriented." What if we viewed church as a vehicle for change in our lives and in our kids' lives? What if we went on a mission to find that sticky web of relationships for our children? What if we were willing to be part of another family's web? Take a step back and think about how going deeper in church and other organizations can help build powerful intergenerational relationships.

ENGAGE THE LOCAL CHURCH IN WORLDVIEW EQUIPPING

Biblical worldview training, sorting through curriculum issues, taking time to understand your rights in the public school system— let's be honest, this does not sound like a pleasure cruise. As we say in our seminars, how many of us after a long day of work or parenting want to curl up with a good book on the cosmological argument for God or the legal history of religious expression in public schools? Stephen and I are passionate about these topics, yet even we, in our busy parenting season of life, have a hard time focusing on our own equipping. It is critical to involve other Christians.

You can have a large influence on how seriously your church takes worldview equipping. Churches generally want to hear feedback from their members. Pastors and lay leaders are often pulled in many different directions, so pray about being willing to spearhead the organization of a Biblical worldview event or small group (like our series called Standing Firm). You could also host a seminar on navigating public schools or on specific curriculum issues. If pastors know a topic is important to you, they are often willing to invest resources to help. Here are some suggestions of how to involve others in your church in worldview-equipping and navigating public schools:

- Organize a seminar series or weekend event
- Suggest a Sunday school topic

- Organize a parenting seminar during youth group
- Offer a movie/documentary night at church about a topic you are passionate about
- Attend a conference along with other parents and/or kids in a youth group
- Host a book club
- Brainstorm with your pastor about these issues and how to take action

We'd love to help you in this area. Please see our website (www.PrepareTheWay.us) for more ideas, and please contact us to discuss other ways we can help you.

CONNECT WITH CAMPUS CHRISTIAN GROUPS

We should all be thankful that several key Christian leaders listened, years ago, to the call God placed on their lives and so started many very effective campus Christian organizations. Jesse Irvin Overholtzer founded Child Evangelism Fellowship in 1937. Consider his inspiring story: "Growing up in a religious family, Jesse at the age of 12 was convicted of his own sin and sought counsel from his mother. He was told, 'Son, you are too young.' It wasn't until Overholtzer was in college that he heard the Gospel and trusted Christ as his Savior. Later as a pastor Mr. Overholtzer read one of Charles Spurgeon's sermons which stated, 'A child of five, if properly instructed can as truly believe and be regenerated as an adult.' The Lord used this statement in Mr. O's life to lead him to begin the ministry of Child Evangelism Fellowship when he was 60 years old. The ministry has grown into the largest evangelistic outreach to children in the world. CEF is currently ministering in over 187 countries and in every state in the U.S. with over 40,000 volunteers."[5] I (Stephen) started a CEF Good News Club at the school where I was a teacher. Because the club met after school hours, it did not violate my contract not to proselytize. Immediately after the bell rang, I could legally hand out Bibles, share the gospel, and pray with my students in the club.

---

[5] http://www.cefonline.com/

What we have seen again and again in our ministry is that students who are involved in campus Christian groups have a vastly higher chance of sticking with their faith. We would also add that many students need parental help in finding out information on Christian groups. Do not expect your student to be mature or motivated enough to research these organizations. Find out which groups are active at the school or college where your student is attending and when they meet. Make contact with the leaders. Obviously, you know the dynamics of your relationship and how much you can gently prod. We know that parental pushing often backfires, but presenting information and encouragement is often needed.

Here is a list of organizations you should check out in an effort to help your student find the right fit:

- Child Evangelism Fellowship (Elementary School, www.cefonline.com)
- WyldLife (Middle School, organized by Young Life, www.younglife.org)
- Young Life (High School, www.younglife.org)
- Fellowship of Christian Athletes (Middle and High School, www.fca.org)
- InterVarsity Christian Fellowship (College, www.intervarsity.org)
- Campus Crusade for Christ (now called CRU, College, www.cru.org)
- American Heritage Girls (Ages 5–18, www.americanheritagegirls.org)
- Trail Life (Ages 5–21, www.traillifeusa.com)

Sometimes people let one bad experience with a particular person or organization along the way hinder their willingness to "join the armada." Because we all have a sinful nature, hurts will happen. We should expect this and pray for wisdom when it does. To never have conflict is an unrealistic expectation. We must be willing to forgive, learn, reconcile, don't let hard situations stop us, and keep in mind that we (and our children) will miss out if we don't.

Not only can there be great benefits for your children to connect with campus ministry groups, it can be a fulfilling ministry field for you. You may find in this season that this is just the kind of ministry you have been longing for. For example, we have had several experiences where parents and teachers have attended our seminars, heard about CEF Good News Clubs, and then pursued starting a club in their children's school or the school where they teach. These ministry fields have been an enormous blessing for them.

Pursue Praying with Others

Romans 12:12 gives good advice when it comes to facing challenges: "Be joyful in hope, patient in affliction, faithful in prayer." First Thessalonians 5:16–18 delivers a similar reminder: "Be joyful always; pray continually; give thanks in all circumstances, for this is God's will for you in Christ Jesus." Simply put, do not miss out on the blessing, encouragement, and power that come from having the mind of Christ! Prayer is central to this mindset. It sounds simple, but too many Christians neglect to pray, or do not believe their prayers are heard. Praying with other Christians can help motivate us in our prayer lives. Lift your children and your schools up in prayer with your spouse, home group, and discipleship groups.

There are several organizations that specifically focus on praying for schools. We have been very impressed by a non-profit organization called Moms in Prayer. Their mission statement reads, "Moms in Prayer International impacts children and schools worldwide for Christ by gathering mothers to pray."[6] Consider joining or starting a Moms in Prayer group at your school.

See You at the Pole organizes a day of prayer at school flagpoles around the globe every September and also organizes a week of prayer around the same time.[7] See You at the Pole started as a tiny, simple, grassroots effort by ten students in 1990 but has grown into an international movement. Find people at your child's school to pray with you, and encourage others to do the same. You won't be sorry you did!

---

[6] https://www.momsinprayer.org/
[7] http://syatp.com/

Consider Fern Nichols's (founder of Mom's In Prayer) testimony on the power of prayer.

> In the fall of 1984, Fern Nichols' two eldest children were entering junior high school. Her heart was heavy and burdened with concern as she knew they would be facing their greatest test in resisting immoral values, vulgar language, peer pressure and philosophies that could undermine their faith. She cried out to the Lord asking Him to protect them, to enable them to see clearly the difference between right and wrong, and to make good decisions. The burden to intercede for her boys was overwhelming. She asked God to give her another mom who felt the same burden, and who would be willing to pray with her concerning their children and their school. God heard the cry of her heart and led her to another mom who shared her burden. Others were invited to come, and they began meeting the following week for prayer. In 1987, she moved and once again she prayed that God would raise up moms who were willing to "stand in the gap" for their children . . . Soon many other groups began to form for schools in her school district. This grassroots effort spread quickly as moms prayed for groups to start around the state and across the nation . . . Today, Moms in Prayer International has groups in every state in the USA and in more than 140 countries worldwide.

Do you have a burden for your children to stand firm in their faith? Then be intentional about praying for them and crying out to God to help them stand up for truth in an increasingly hostile culture.

In this chapter, we have included a number of different avenues to enable you to connect with other Christians on the journey of navigating your public schools. Pray for God's wisdom, then start today to expand your community; you will be blessed. Community is never perfect, because people are not perfect. Keep that in mind and extend grace to others. He might lead you to finally take that step of commitment and join a local church or small group. Or He might lead you to start a Moms in Prayer group in your child's school. Not only are we more encouraged when we are part of a supportive community, but we can then use our own spiritual gifts for a greater purpose. The Bible is very clear that we are not meant to journey alone.

CHAPTER 5

THE "SEPARATION OF CHURCH AND STATE" SHIPWRECK

> But the greatest injury of the "wall" notion is its mischievous diversion of judges from the actual intentions of the drafters of the Bill of Rights . . . The "wall of separation between church and State" is a metaphor based on bad history, a metaphor which has proved useless as a guide to judging. It should be frankly and explicitly abandoned.
>
> —Supreme Court Chief Justice Williams Rehnquist, 1985

The misinterpretation of the phrase "separation of church and state" has permeated our culture and has robbed many parents and students of their willingness to live out their faith in public schools. Most Christians are being shipwrecked by this tragically misleading metaphor.

The reality is that while we have lost ground in the area of freedom of religion in the past fifty years, Christians have far more rights to live out their faith in public schools than they think. These fundamental rights are openly enshrined in the First Amendment to the U.S. Constitution, yet most people involved in the public schools do not even know these rights exist! The misinterpretation of the separation of church and state is 1) preventing students from freely living out the gospel in schools, 2) causing children to be ashamed of their Christian faith, and 3) influencing teachers to wrongly censor Christian references in curriculum in favor of secular political correctness. Our desire is to empower Christians to know and utilize their First Amendment rights in order to protect a Biblical worldview, and also to influence their schools with the gospel of Jesus Christ.

Most people have heard the phrase "separation of church and state," yet they will flounder when asked how the First Amendment of the U.S. Constitution impacts their freedom of religion. How could a phrase such as "the separation of church and state" (which is not even in the Constitution) garner so much attention, while the First Amendment collects dust in the American consciousness? For all practical purposes, the false notion of separation of church and state has replaced the U.S. Constitution in many people's minds. There has been a very successful agenda that has accomplished this mission.

Numerous parents mistakenly think that their children cannot bring Bibles or Christian books to school to read during free reading time or recess, due to the separation of church and state. Some students have come to me and said that they cannot invite friends at school to church activities for fear of getting in trouble. This often leaves children ashamed of their church involvement. One boy came to us after he was reprimanded by a teacher for handing out flyers to his church's skateboard park because of . . . you guessed it, separation of church and state. After talking with the principal and explaining the student's First Amendment rights, he was then able to hand out his flyers.

This topic also greatly affects teachers. As I described earlier, my principal used the infamous separation of church and state phrase to censor my use of primary source documents with Christian references. I have met numerous teachers who completely avoid the topic of Christianity in planning their curriculum, even when it relates to the standards. Meanwhile, teachers feel fairly free to share about religions other than Christianity. As a result, the separation of church and state has in many schools turned into separation of Christianity and state. When it comes to other religions, there is a prevailing double standard: teachers are applauded for being culturally diverse when incorporating other faiths in their curriculum, but are rebuked for violating the alleged "separation of church and state" when the topic of Christianity comes up in the classroom.

FIRST AMENDMENT V. "SEPARATION OF CHURCH AND STATE"

The U.S. Constitution was written in 1787. It is the foundation of our American government. The first ten amendments to the Constitution, clarifying vital rights of U.S. citizens, are called the Bill of Rights. These amendments were so crucial that the Constitution would never have been ratified if it had not included these key rights—in particular the First Amendment, which guarantees freedom of religion. Understanding what the First Amendment of the U.S. Constitution says about your freedom of religion will help you and your children exercise your rights in public schools. It is noteworthy that our freedom of religion is established in the very *first* of the ten amendments that constitute the Bill of Rights. Securing freedom of religion was clearly an important goal for the Founders; that they listed this important right first, shows that they valued this right above the others. Many people wrongly think that the U.S. Constitution contains the phrase "separation of church and state." It doesn't. In reality, the Constitution secures your freedom of religion.

We will discuss the origin of this phrase later in this chapter. First, though, we will start by looking at the portions of the First Amendment that deal directly with religion: these portions are often called the Establishment Clause and the Free Exercise Clause.

> Congress shall make no law respecting an establishment of religion, or prohibiting the free exercise thereof.[1]

Up to the first comma of this phrase is the Establishment Clause; after it comes the Free Exercise clause. So what does this mean? In reading the public debates that took place in Congress, as well as the early writings of key government officials, we can see that the Founders were trying to prevent a government-sponsored denomination of Christianity, such as the Anglican Church in

---

[1] The full text reads: "Congress shall make no law respecting an establishment of religion, or prohibiting the free exercise thereof; or abridging the freedom of speech, or of the press; or the right of the people peaceably to assemble, and to petition the Government for a redress of grievances."

England. They wanted to be free to practice any denomination of Christianity they chose, whether Baptist or Anglican or any other. In their day the Bible was the main textbook used in public schools, prayer was common in government meetings, and they even held Christian church services in Congress; so clearly the Founders did not feel any of these practices violated the Establishment Clause.

The Founders' intent was not a complete separation of church and state as understood by our culture today. Reading the transcripts of the debates recorded in Congress during the drafting of the First Amendment gives insight into its intended meaning. James Madison, a key Founder and responsible for the addition of the Bill of Rights to our Constitution, initially suggested the following:

"The civil rights of none shall be abridged on account of religious belief or worship, nor shall any national religion be established."
"Congress shall not make any law, infringing the rights of conscience or establishing any Religious Sect or Society," (the word "sect" in those days meant any one denomination of Christianity).
"Congress shall make no law establishing any particular denomination of religion in preference to another, or prohibiting the free exercise thereof, nor shall the rights of conscience be infringed."
"Congress shall make no law establishing articles of faith, or a mode of worship, or prohibiting the free exercise of religion."
Final wording approved Sept 28, 1789: "Congress shall make no law respecting an establishment of religion, or prohibiting the free exercise thereof . . . "

Furthermore, it is an interesting bit of history that one of the key authors of the Establishment Clause, Fisher Ames, in 1801 said this:

> [Why] should not the Bible regain the place it once held as a school book? Its morals are pure, its examples captivating and noble. The reverence for the Sacred Book that is thus early impressed lasts long.

As mentioned earlier, Fisher Ames was a signer of the Declaration of Independence; he also played a crucial role in drafting the wording of the Establishment Clause. He clearly did not feel that using the Bible as a key part of all public school curricula infringed upon the Establishment Clause. Fisher Ames was noting at the turn of the century that some other textbooks, besides the Bible, were being taught in public schools and the result was that some schools were not focusing as much time on the Bible. How ironic that he wanted to secure the Bible's place in public school curriculum!

Supreme Court Justice Joseph Story, considered the father of our American legal system, gave insight into the original intent of the Founders.

> We are not to attribute this [First Amendment] prohibition of a national religious establishment to an indifference to religion in general, and especially to Christianity (which none could hold in more reverence, than the framers of the Constitution) . . . Probably, at the time of the adoption of the Constitution, and of the Amendment to it now under consideration, the general if not the universal, sentiment in America was that Christianity ought to receive encouragement from the State . . . Any attempt to level all religions and to make it a matter of state policy to hold all in utter indifference would have created universal disapprobation [disapproval] if not universal indignation.[2]

Consider what the House and Senate Judiciary Committee reports on the Establishment Clause said in 1853–1854:

> What is an establishment of religion? It must have a creed defining what a man must believe; it must have rites and ordinances which believers must observe; it must have ministers of defined qualifications to teach the doctrines and administer the rites; it must have tests for the submissive and penalties for the nonconformist. There never was an established religion without all these . . . Had the people, during the Revolution, had a suspicion of any attempt to war against Christianity, that Revolution would have been strangled in its cradle. **At the time of the adoption of the Constitution and the amendments, the universal sentiment was that Christianity should be encouraged,** not any one sect [denomination]. Any attempt to level and discard all

---

[2] Supreme Court Justice Joseph Story, *Commentaries on the Constitution*, 1833

religion would have been viewed with universal indignation . . . It [Christianity] must be considered as the foundation on which the whole structure rests. In this age there can be no substitution for Christianity; that, in its general principles, is the great conservative element on which we must rely for the purity and permanence of free institutions. That was the religion of the founders of the republic, and they expected it to remain the religion of their descendents.[3] [emphasis added]

The Senate Judiciary Committee was in agreement with the House Judiciary Committee:

The clause speaks of "an establishment of religion." What is meant by that expression? It referred, without doubt, to the establishment which existed in the mother-country . . . [The Founders] intended, by the Amendment, to prohibit 'an establishment of religion' such as the English Church presented, or any thing like it. But they had no fear or jealousy of religion itself, nor did they wish to see us an irreligious people . . . they did not intend to spread over all the public authorities and the whole public action of the nation the dead and revolting spectacle of atheistical apathy.[4]

The Founders clearly did not intend for the First Amendment to result in a complete separation of religion and government. President John Adams considered Christian principles so important to the proper functioning of American society that he said in a 1798 presidential address:

We have no government armed with power capable of contending with human passions unbridled by morality and religion . . . Our constitution was made only for a moral and religious people. It is wholly inadequate to the government of any other.

President Adams knew that, without Christian principles helping to transform the citizens from within, from the heart, our government was wholly inadequate to govern the citizens from the outside. In fact, this was a common thought among most of the founders. George Washington said on September 17, 1796 in his Farewell Address:

---

[3] U.S. House of Representatives, *Judiciary Committee Report on Religion*, 1854
[4] U.S. Senate, *Judiciary Committee Report on the Establishment Clause*, 1853

> Let it simply be asked, Where is the security for property, for reputation, for life, if the sense of religious obligation desert . . .? And let us with caution indulge the supposition that morality can be maintained without religion. Whatever may be conceded to the influence of refined education on minds . . . reason and experience both forbid us to expect that national morality can prevail, in exclusion of religious principle.

The citizens of a nation are either guided by an internal morality or controlled by an external legal system. Robert Winthrop, Speaker of the House and also a U.S. Senator, said this, "Men, in a word, must necessarily be controlled either by a power within them or by a power without them; either by the Word of God or by the strong arm of man; either by the Bible or by the bayonet." For the first two hundred years of our nation, most citizens were restrained by an internal belief in Judeo-Christian morality. Founder John Witherspoon, member of the Continental Congress and a signer of the Declaration, realized that when Christians are living out their faith by loving God and loving their neighbors, society as a whole benefits:

> Virtue and piety are inseparably connected; then to promote true religion is the best and most effectual way of making a virtuous and regular people. Love to God and love to man is the substance of religion; when these prevail, civil laws will have little to do.[5]

Even Thomas Jefferson, who was one of the least religious of the Founders, referenced the teachings of Jesus as the appropriate plumb line for our nation's moral code:

> The practice of morality being necessary for the well-being of society, He [God] has taken care to impress its precepts so indelibly on our hearts that they shall not be effaced by the subtleties of our brain. We all agree in the obligation of the moral precepts of Jesus and nowhere will they be found delivered in greater purity than in His discourses.[6]

---

[5] John Witherspoon, *Works*, 1815

[6] Thomas Jefferson, "Letter to James Fishback," September 27, 1809, *The Writings of Thomas Jefferson*

Unfortunately, many people in our nation today have had their conscience seared. Our nation's moral compass has been replaced for the most part by secularism and moral relativism. Founder James Otis said, "When a man's will and pleasure is his only rule and guide, what safety can there be either for him or against him but in the point of a sword?" Otis recognized the danger of relativistic morality, which tends to result in people simply choosing their own personal "will and pleasure." Crime has skyrocketed in the last fifty years because we have forsaken the most effective force that restrains people, which is God's unchanging truth.

Consider what David Barton concluded in his book *Original Intent*:

> Disregarding these direct societal benefits which result from the promotion of religious principles, government utilizes extensive manpower and expends massive financial sums attempting to restrain behavior which is the external manifestation of internal chaos and disorder. If human behavior is not controlled by the internal restraints provided through religion [Judeo-Christian morality], then the only other means to restrain misbehavior is the threat of sheer force.[7]

The majority of the Founders agreed that citizens needed to be restrained by a force from within them and they encouraged Judeo-Christian morality at all levels of government, and in all areas of society and culture. Only in the last several decades have we seen our society's Judeo-Christian moral compass replaced with secularism and moral relativism. We are seeing the resulting moral decay. Signer of the Declaration and influential Founder Dr. Benjamin Rush said,

> In contemplating the political institutions of the United States, I lament that we waste so much time and money in punishing crimes, and take so little pains to prevent them. We profess to be Republicans and yet we neglect the only means of establishing

---

[7] David Barton, *Original Intent: The Courts, The Constitution, and Religion*, Wallbuilder Press, 2013. David Barton of Wallbuilders has done outstanding work in this area of educating Americans on the Christian moorings of the nation. I would encourage everyone to make use of the extensive resources he has available on his website, www.wallbuilders.com

and perpetuating our republican forms of government; that is, the universal education of our youth in the principles of Christianity by means of the Bible.[8]

George Washington rebuked those who would subvert Christian morality:

> Of all the dispositions and habits which lead to political prosperity, religion and morality are indispensable supports. In vain would that man claim the tribute of patriotism who should labor to subvert these great pillars of human happiness.[9]

In our modern culture there are many who are actively subverting the morality that our nation was founded upon, yet many Christians are not motivated to act. By their inaction, Christians are actually part of that subversion of Christian morals. As Daniel Webster warned almost prophetically, "Our destruction, if it come at all, will be from the inattention of the people to the concerns of their government, from their carelessness and negligence."[10]

It is precisely Christian principles that the Founders nearly universally agreed were the foundation, the mooring, on which America rests. They knew that if those religious moorings were lost, we would indeed be a nation adrift, as we find ourselves today.[11]

THE ORIGIN OF THE PHRASE "SEPARATION OF CHURCH AND STATE"

The words "separation of church and state" are not found in the Constitution, Bill of Rights, or any other Founding document, yet most Americans today are more familiar with this phrase than they are the First Amendment. Where did this phrase come from? It originally came from a previously obscure letter that Thomas Jefferson wrote to a group of Baptists in Danbury, Connecticut in 1802. The Baptists were concerned that Jefferson, an Episcopalian

---

[8] Benjamin Rush, *Essays*, "Defense of the Use of the Bible as a School Book"
[9] George Washington, "Farewell Address," 1796
[10] Daniel Webster, *The Works of Daniel Webster*, 1840
[11] For more on this topic, see the excellent documentary by New Liberty Videos, "A Nation Adrift," http://www.christiananswers.net/catalog/nation-vs.html

(from the Church of England), would select his denomination of Christianity as the state-sponsored denomination in America. They were concerned that Baptists might be persecuted by the federal government just as they had been persecuted by the Church of England. After all, many of the Founders had come to America to escape persecution of their religious denomination by the Church of England. Fear of government persecution is what spurred the Danbury Baptists to write to President Jefferson. They were concerned that the Church of England was about to become the Church of America. In his letter of reply to the Danbury Baptists, Jefferson assures the Baptists that they have no need to fear the government getting involved in their religious matters, because:

> I contemplate with sovereign reverence that act of the whole American people which declared that their legislature should "make no law respecting an establishment of religion or prohibiting the free exercise thereof," thus building a wall of separation between Church and State.[12]

This obscure letter by Jefferson, which was never cited in any Founding documents nor in any court decisions until later in the twentieth century, is the only source of the so-called "separation of church and state" language. In fact, Jefferson also wrote in another letter that the government was prohibited from interfering in *any and all* religious exercises.

> I consider the government of the United States as interdicted [prohibited] by the Constitution from intermeddling with religious institutions . . . or exercises.[13]

Jefferson would have considered voluntary Scripture reading or prayer in schools a religious exercise protected by the Constitution. His letter to the Danbury Baptists did not influence our government much until 1947, when a court decision (which quoted this phrase) took it completely out of context. The purpose of the Establishment Clause is actually to *protect* religious institutions and public religious exercises from government control. Yet, with the current misapplication of the phrase "separation of church and state," we are falsely led to believe that it is Congress's

---

[12] Thomas Jefferson, "Letter to the Danbury Baptists," 1802
[13] Thomas Jefferson, "Letter to Samuel Miller," 1808

responsibility to *restrict* religious expression in all areas of government and culture. This is so far removed from the original intent of the Establishment Clause that it has in fact flipped the intent of the First Amendment on its head![14]

The late Supreme Court Justice William Rehnquist had the most succinct and to the point description of the so-called separation of church and state. He referred to it as "a misleading metaphor":

> But the greatest injury of the "wall" notion is its mischievous diversion of judges from the actual intentions of the drafters of the Bill of Rights . . . The "wall of separation between church and State" is a metaphor based on bad history, a metaphor which has proved useless as a guide to judging. It should be frankly and explicitly abandoned.[15]

What was originally intended to *prevent* Congress from interfering with religious institutions or exercises has only recently been misinterpreted as meaning that Congress must *restrict* religious exercises. As we have seen, nothing could be further from the original intent of the Founders.

THE ROAD TO "SEPARATION OF CHURCH AND STATE" AS WE KNOW IT

What led to this "misleading metaphor," as Justice Rehnquist called it? Let's look at some of the court decisions that have led to our modern misunderstanding of the separation of church and state. The first case in which the Supreme Court took Jefferson's phrase out of context, applying an entirely new meaning to it, was the 1947 case of *Everson v. Board of Education*. This was the first misapplication of the alleged "wall of separation."

Justice Hugo Black, a devout anti-Catholic, wrote a decision in which he declared, "The First Amendment has erected a wall between church and state. That wall must be kept high and impregnable. We could not approve the slightest breach."

---

[14] David Barton, *Original Intent*
[15] Chief Justice William H. Rehnquist, *Wallace v. Jaffree*, U.S. Supreme Court, 1985

For nearly 300 years of our nation's history, Christianity was encouraged at all levels of society and government. The First Amendment was 1) intended to keep Congress from establishing one denomination of Christianity and 2) to stop government from meddling in religious institutions and exercises. But in 1947, the Supreme Court flipped the intended meaning of the First Amendment on its head. Thus began the federal government's un-Constitutional restriction of our religious rights.

The next case on the road to the restriction of religious freedom in America occurred in 1948 in *McCollum v. Board of Education*. In this case the Supreme Court banned voluntary, parent-authorized, elective classes in religion because they were paid for with government funds. With the increase in jurisdiction that the reinterpreted First Amendment gave the courts, they started to flex their judicial usurpation of power using this recently acquired misleading metaphor:[16]

- 1962 School-sponsored prayers to start the day declared un-Constitutional
- 1963 School-led Scripture reading in class is not allowed
- 1980 Ten Commandments, standing alone, cannot be displayed in schools
- 1985 Moment of silence specifically for prayer declared un-Constitutional
- 1989 Un-Constitutional to display nativity scene on public land by itself
- 1993 Ten Commandments can't be displayed at courthouses
- 1993 Religious artwork by itself may not be displayed at school
- 2000 Barring school-endorsed, student-led prayer at school sporting events

Through a simplified description of these court cases, you can see the trend. The federal judiciary has consistently expanded its influence and control over more and more areas of American society, and over the practice and expression of religious beliefs

---

[16] David Barton, *Original Intent*

by American citizens. The result has been to remove or severely restrict our religious freedoms: freedoms that are guaranteed to us by the U.S. Constitution.

How do you think the Founders would feel about this misleading metaphor and how it has been distorted? Would they be upset that the freedom of religion they fought so long and hard to secure has been redefined almost out of existence? I'm convinced of it.

The Founders would also be upset because they provided a way in which "we the people," could legally change any part of the Constitution if we desired to do so. It is called an amendment. In Article 5 of the Constitution, the Founders spelled out how to amend the Constitution; it is only to be done by a decision of the people. If we wanted to secularize our society, the Constitution allows that, by a decision of the people, we could write and vote on an amendment saying that we want a more secular nation. However, this is not the way the First Amendment has been changed.

Would the founders be upset at the *way* the Establishment Clause has been redefined? Absolutely! They never intended for the judiciary to be able to change the Constitution just because they want to. Pick any issue today, and odds are the judiciary has meddled where they never were intended to. George Washington had this to say in 1796 in his Farewell Address:

> If, in the opinion of the people, the distribution or the modification of the constitutional powers be in any particular wrong, let it be corrected by an amendment in the way which the Constitution designates. But let there be no change by *usurpation* [wrongful seizure of power]; for though this, in one instance, may be the instrument of good, it is the customary weapon by which free governments are destroyed. [emphasis added]

The federal judiciary has usurped powers which they were never intended to have. The separation of church and state as we know it has been imposed on us by their wrongful abuse of power and by anti-religious groups like the American Civil Liberties Union and the Freedom from Religion Foundation pushing the false claim that religion has no place in our schools. The consequences are vast, and they pervasively impact our children in public schools.

Fortunately, although voluntary prayer, Scripture reading, and acknowledgment of the Ten Commandments have been severely restricted by the judicial branch's usurping of power, the First Amendment still guarantees you and your children the freedom to express and practice your religious beliefs, even in public schools. Many Christians think that a total separation of religion and state has been established. This is not the case! We should not give more ground than has already been taken. It is crucial that you understand the rights you and your children still have under the First Amendment. The following chapters should empower you to understand and exercise those rights.

CHAPTER 6

TAKE THE SHIP'S WHEEL: KNOW YOUR RIGHTS

The state may not establish a "religion of secularism" in the sense of affirmatively opposing or showing hostility to religion, thus "preferring those who believe in no religion over those who do believe." Refusal to permit religious exercises thus is seen, not as the realization of state neutrality, but rather as the establishment of a religion of secularism.

—U.S. Supreme Court, *Abington Township v. Schempp* (1963)

It can hardly be argued that either students or teachers shed their constitutional rights to freedom of speech or expression at the schoolhouse gate.

—U.S. Supreme Court, *Tinker v. Des Moines School District* (1969)

When you understand your rights, you are better empowered to exercise them. Too often, parents hand over the ship's wheel. So we will begin this chapter by summarizing your rights in public schools. This is the practical heart of what you can and cannot do; it is vital to understand these rights if you and your children are to navigate through public school effectively.

The first several sections of this chapter describe the legal rights of parents, students, teachers, staff members, and extra-curricular groups in public schools. We hope that as a result of reading this chapter you can be more of a Christian presence and a light for Christ in the public school system. One section of this chapter aims to clarify a misunderstood topic by making the distinction between *rights before God* (which we do *not* have) and *rights in relation to other humans* (which God *gives* us). We want to point out that it is crucial to exercise your rights with a heart of Christian love towards all those around you. As Paul points out in First Corinthians 13, we may be right, but our "rightness" will sound like a clanging gong or clashing cymbal if we do not communicate in love. May we be graceful as we put this information into practice.

Rights of Parents and Students

Our rights as human beings and as parents ultimately come from God. If you are a parent, God has blessed you with children and has given you the responsibility to "train them up in the way they should go." Mathew Staver, in his book *Eternal Vigilance*, says this: "In reality, parental rights are not derived from or created by the United States Constitution. Rather, parental rights derive from natural law, what the Declaration of Independence refers to as 'unalienable rights' with which we are endowed by our Creator."[1] Mat is also the founder and chairman of Liberty Counsel, a Christian legal firm protecting religious liberty. Their website contains outstanding resources.[2] When we understand that our rights come from God, it gives us proper perspective: that as Christians we are, first and foremost, called to be obedient to Biblical principles.

However, according to Romans 13, the Bible also instructs us to follow our society's laws, as long as they do not contradict a Biblical worldview. God established governments to protect those that do good and punish evildoers. According to Romans 13, "Everyone must submit himself to the governing authorities, for there is no authority except that which God has established.

---

[1] Mathew Staver, *Eternal Vigilance: Knowing and Protecting Your Religious Freedom*, Broadman & Holman, 2005
[2] www.LC.org

The authorities that exist have been established by God . . . For rulers hold no terror for those who do right, but for those who do wrong . . . But if you do wrong, be afraid, for he does not bear the sword for nothing. He is God's servant, an agent of wrath to bring punishment on the wrongdoer."

The only place where right and wrong are fully and clearly defined is in the Bible. But unless our government's laws violate Biblical principles, we are called as Christians to also operate within the legal framework of our society. Thankfully, parents and students actually have many more rights than they think! Many parents we have encountered do not realize that they have significant rights within the public school system. In the case *Pierce v. Society of Sisters,* the U.S. Supreme Court described this parental authority:

> The fundamental theory of liberty upon which all governments in this Union repose excludes any general power of the state to standardize its children by forcing them to accept instruction from public teachers only. The child is not the mere creature of the state.

This ruling means that parents should consider themselves their children's most important teacher. In a nutshell, a parent has the right to ensure that his or her child's Biblical worldview is not being discriminated against by school officials. Parents also have legal authority to request that their child be removed from any lesson or activity that violates their religious beliefs. Many parents are afraid that if they pull a student from a lesson, the child may suffer from persecution by teachers or students. If that were to happen, parents also have the right to address the issue with the principal, and ultimately, the school board. A wonderful national organization which helps parents understand their God-given rights to be in charge of educating their children is Parental Rights.[3]

A student also has the right to incorporate his or her Christian faith in school.[4] As noted above, the Supreme Court ruled in *Tinker v. Des Moines School District* that "it can hardly be argued that either students or teachers shed their constitutional rights to freedom of

---

[3] www.ParentalRights.org
[4] See Appendix C for more rights of students

speech or expression at the schoolhouse gate." Our federal government has written several documents clearly defining the many appropriate ways that Christians can live out their faith in public schools. From the Federal Department of Education's "Guidelines on Religious Expression in Public Schools" comes this quote:

> Students may express their beliefs about religion in the form of homework, artwork, and other written and oral assignments free of discrimination based on the religious content of their submissions.[5]

In other words, students are allowed to incorporate their faith and worldview into *all* curricular areas, from writing to art to science.[6] For example, during show-and-tell, not only may elementary school students bring a Bible to show and discuss—they can also share about details of the Christian faith and why it is important to them. If a teacher or administrator were to tell the child that they are not allowed to share about Christianity or the Bible, that would actually be an illegal violation of the student's Constitutional rights! (This violation is called *viewpoint discrimination*.) If a high school student is participating in a speech and debate class and they are giving a persuasive speech on abortion, they have a Constitutionally protected right to discuss the topic from a religious, moral point of view and to encourage others to share their view. Or if a middle school student is writing a paper on a historical figure, they can write about the Apostle Paul and use the Bible as a source. As long as students follow the teacher's directions for the assignment, they should get a good grade. If they get a poor grade based on the content (a common issue when it comes to matters of faith), it is a violation of the student's rights and should be addressed using the appropriate channels of authority (see chapter 11). The U.S. Department of Education clearly states in this regard, "if a teacher's assignment involves writing a poem, the work of a student who submits a poem in the form of a prayer (for example, a psalm) should be judged on the basis of academic standards (such as literary quality) and neither

---

[5] U.S. Department of Education, "Religious Expression in Public Schools," *See* Appendix A

[6] See also Appendix C

penalized nor rewarded on account of its religious content."[7] (See the appendices for more on these guidelines.)

As you can see, the guidelines that the federal government has already established are *very* empowering for Christians. Here's another excerpt on student's rights:

> Among other things, students may read their Bibles or other scriptures, say grace before meals, and pray or study religious materials with fellow students during recess, the lunch hour, or other non-instructional time to the same extent that they may engage in nonreligious activities."[8]

Students may bring Bibles to school and read them during free reading time and may reference their faith in written assignments, projects, and speeches. Basically, the U.S. Constitution and the U.S. Department of Education permit Christians to openly incorporate and express their religious beliefs in *all* curricular areas.

But many teachers and administrators are not aware of these religious freedoms in public school settings, so it is important for parents to know these rights and the organizations that can clarify and explain their rights to them. For example, Andrew Raker, a student at Millbrook High School in Winchester, Virginia, was reprimanded by school officials and prevented from sharing a pro-life message during the national annual "Pro-Life Day of Silent Solidarity." He called the Christian legal group Alliance Defending Freedom (ADF) to ask if this was legal. ADF got the decision overturned and commented, "Hopefully schools elsewhere will also recognize that students are not stripped of their First Amendment right to pro-life speech when they enter the schoolhouse gate."[9]

In addition to having parental rights that enable one to direct their child's education, parents also have many freedoms as a volunteer on school campuses. Schools regularly rely on the help of volunteers and are often very open to outside help. This can include helping in the classroom with the students, but it can also consist of helping at any level of school operations: library assistance, afterschool tutors, administrative volunteers, science fair

---

[7] U.S. Department of Education, "Guidance on Constitutionally Protected Prayer in Public Elementary and Secondary Schools," See Appendix B
[8] Ibid.
[9] Alliance Defending Freedom, News Release, 2007

coordinators, organizing extra-curricular activities, etc. A parent or volunteer can sometimes share about their faith more freely than a staff member can. Volunteers can also be pastors from the community. They can help in a variety of ways and are allowed to express their faith at appropriate times. For example, a pastor in our church felt called to help the students at a local elementary school. He asked the principal if they needed help mentoring at-risk students. The school enthusiastically accepted his help. He has developed outstanding relationships with some of the children who were really struggling at school. He has even been able to share many Christian truths, and a parent has started to become involved in our church. Though there are some restrictions for volunteers incorporating their faith on public school campuses, they have considerable freedoms in this area. Another pastor friend of ours was allowed to share—in his daughter's classroom—about the true meaning of Christmas and what the holiday means to him personally. This was a situation where a teacher would have to be very careful about sharing his or her personal faith, but the parent volunteer had fewer restrictions.

In summary, students have great freedom to speak and live out their Christian faith in public schools.[10] They also have a Constitutionally protected right to incorporate their beliefs in all curricular areas, free from discrimination, as long as it is relevant to the topic or assignment. Parents and volunteers are slightly more restricted in living out their faith in schools, but still have substantial freedoms. We encourage everyone involved in public schools to exercise and steward these rights in a graceful way that shines the light of Christ in the school system.

Rights of Teachers and Staff Members

Teachers and paid staff also have many more rights than they may realize.[11] One of the most confusing areas for the teachers we know is when it is appropriate or not to include the topic of Christianity in the classroom. Many teachers, especially Christian

---

[10] See also Appendix A, B, C, and E
[11] See Appendix D on Teacher's Rights

teachers, are afraid to even mention God or the Christian religion. Yet this avoidance will either 1) establish a "religion of secularism" as the Supreme Court says, or 2) create a bias towards other religions. It is clear from the law that teachers may not proselytize (try to convert) during school hours or during time periods when they are on the job. However, this does not at all mean that they need to avoid the name of God or Jesus altogether.

As far as what teachers may legally include in their classroom curriculum, they need not fear mentioning Christianity as long as it is appropriate for the content standards. There are many appropriate places where Christianity naturally comes up in content standards. The Federal Department of Education says this:

> Public schools may not provide religious instruction, but they may teach about religion, including the Bible or other scripture: the history of religion, comparative religion, the Bible (or other scripture)-as-literature, and the role of religion in the history of the United States.[12]

For example, a teacher has a Constitutionally protected right to teach about Christianity, and to use the Bible as the central piece in a literature assignment or the role of religion in the history of the United States. As we've seen from previous chapters, we indeed have a rich Christian heritage. What we have found while talking to Christian teachers is that they are often so cautious about being accused of violating the Establishment Clause, that they almost avoid mentioning anything to do with Christianity. However, this is not reflective of the laws of the land or the clear policies that the federal government has already put in place.

What many schools have now developed, because of the prevalent bias against evangelical Christianity, is more of a religion of secularism. This is exactly what the courts have warned against, as described by the Supreme Court:

> The state may not establish a "religion of secularism" in the sense of affirmatively opposing or showing hostility to religion, thus "preferring those who believe in no religion over those who do believe" . . . Refusal to permit religious exercises thus is seen,

---

[12] U.S. Department of Education, "Religious Expression in Public Schools," *See* Appendix A.

not as the realization of state neutrality, but rather as the establishment of a religion of secularism.[13]

What is troubling about the current cultural climate in our school system is that there is a general approval or at least acceptance of this religion of secularism, as well as of a "religion of anything non-Christian." In turn, there is a prevalent disapproval of Christianity. For example, as I experienced and have heard from many other teachers, there are "warm fuzzies" when other religions are taught, but when any mention of Christianity is included in the curriculum, there are quite frequently accusations of "proselytizing." This is why it is important for teachers and administrators to be educated about their rights in the classroom. We include a resource from Alliance Defending Freedom called "The Free Speech and Academic Freedom of Teachers in Public Schools" in Appendix D. Here's an excerpt:

> A teacher may objectively teach the Bible in a history of religions class or study the Bible as part of a literature course. The Bible can be taught in a school for its historical, cultural, or literary value, but not in a devotional or doctrinal manner . . . When studying art, music, drama, or literature a teacher may objectively discuss, perform, critique, and overview religious music, composition, and history . . . a teacher may explain that Easter is a religious holiday celebrated by Christians who believe that the person of Jesus Christ was raised from the dead. Historically, Easter celebrates the resurrection of Christ, whom Christians believe to be God. Done in an objective and educational manner, teachers can speak about religious holidays . . . If the school allows teachers to use its facilities for non-curriculum related matters such as socialization and entertainment, then teachers should also be able to use the same facilities for Bible study and prayer. In this case only teachers should be in the meeting, not students.[14]

As you can see, teachers have many freedoms to appropriately incorporate Christianity in the classroom and even live out their faith on public school campuses. (In a later chapter we discuss how to deal with any conflicts that might come up.)

---

[13] U.S. Supreme Court, *Abington Township v. Schempp*, 1963
[14] See Appendix D.

Employees have certain religious rights in the workplace, and public school employees are no exception. One's workplace is not a "religion-free zone" and employees do not have to leave their faith at home. Federal law prohibits employers and unions from discriminating against an employee's sincerely held religious beliefs. Title VII of the Civil Rights Act of 1964 says,

> It shall be an unlawful employment practice for an employer to fail or refuse to hire or to discharge any individual, or otherwise to discriminate against any individual with respect to his compensation, terms, conditions, or privileges of employment, because of such individual's race, color, religion, sex, or national origin.

If an employee feels that they are facing discrimination based on their faith, there are certain steps they may follow to file an EEOC claim (800 669–3362). The courts have historically ruled in favor of employees in this area.[15] In short, the employee must simply state, verbally and in writing, the sincerely held religious belief that conflicts with their employer's policies. The burden then shifts to the employer to accommodate that belief. Second, the employer must accommodate that religious belief as long as it would not cause an undue hardship.

One invaluable organization for all Christians working in the public school system is the Christian Educators Association International. Their mission is to encourage, equip, and empower educators according to Biblical principles.[16] Teachers, administrators and staff would benefit by joining them; they have a plethora of resources available.

A NOTE ABOUT CHRISTMAS MUSIC IN SCHOOLS

Many teachers, students, and parents frequently ask about singing sacred songs in choirs. This issue arises most often around Christmas. Singing sacred Christmas songs in public school concerts can cause blustery debates. In a cultural climate where

---

[15] See also Appendix D and E.
[16] www.CEAI.org

Nativity displays are removed from public settings with increased frequency, many Christians wonder if sacred Christian songs in choir will be the next to go in their districts. In many cases, they already have—not because it is illegal to sing them in public schools, but simply out of misunderstanding and the fear of legal ramifications. Parents may look sideways at each other when elementary students sweetly sing *Silent Night,* as if someone is doing something terribly wrong. *Is this legal, they wonder?* We hear of cases regarding this topic almost every year.

An interesting case arose here in central Oregon just as we were putting the finishing touches on this book. This was the scenario, according to a local news agency[17]:

> A 15-year-old [High School] student said Friday she is concerned about religious songs in her choir's class and is asking for changes from the school . . . while she loves her class, she does not love the religious songs they're singing. "*Glory to the newborn king,* and then *God and sinners,*" she said, reading the lyrics. Although she grew up in a Christian household, she is not religious herself. "It makes me feel really uncomfortable, because it's not something I want to be singing about, because I don't really believe in it," [she] said . . . "Our teacher says that we can sit out if we feel uncomfortable singing them," [she] said. "I don't think we should be left out of something because they're doing something that's against the law." . . . [She] said she does not mind most Christmas songs, which don't have specific religious references in them. "There is no diversity. I mean, even if they added something about Hanukkah . . . " [she] said.

The news station felt this item warranted headline status: "Another Case of Religion in Public Schools." Here we have a classic case where a student was under the false impression that the school choir singing a Christian song violated "the separation of church and state." The hymn in question was *Hark the Herald Angels Sing,* written by prolific hymn-writer Charles Wesley in 1739. Note the words to this song that the student mentions are about God's plan for reconciliation:

---

[17] Wanda Moore, www.KTVZ.com, "Ridgeview HS student voices concern over sacred songs," Dec. 11, 2015

Hark the herald angels sing
"Glory to the newborn king
Peace on earth and mercy mild
God and sinners reconciled."

Two aspects of this case are common trends. First, the student objected to the *Christ*ian aspect of *Christ*mas, not the secular aspects of Christmas (of which there are many these days). So we are not allowed to even mention the name of Jesus Christ, the true namesake of *Christ*mas? If the culture had its way, the name of the holiday would likely change to *Nick*mas. Those who tend to be disgruntled about Christmas songs are generally fine as long as the namesake is not mentioned and we only focus on Mr. Claus and the North Pole. However, as many choir directors have rightly pointed out, the sacred and historical songs of Christmas are more concerned with celebrating the birth of Christ, the namesake of the holiday. Hence the tension we find in many choir classes.

The second aspect of this case that represents a troubling trend is that the student said she would actually be fine singing about another religion, just not Christianity. Toward the end of the interview, she said she would have felt better singing words about Hanukkah, yet she felt "uncomfortable" with the Christian lyrics. Somehow singing about Hanukkah, which is all about God's faithfulness and provision (to the Jewish Maccabees) is fine, but singing about God's faithfulness and provision of a savior to everyone in the world is not? Students or parents are frequently bothered by Christian references, but not references to other religions. Teachers are applauded for cultural diversity when they include references to other religions, but often when Christianity is mentioned they are under extra scrutiny. This is not "appreciating diversity": this is a double standard.

So can "God and sinners be reconciled" (so to speak) in public schools or not? Was the school doing something "against the law"? The short answer is *no*. Remember, the words "separation of church and state" are not actually in the Constitution or any Founding documents. The choir teacher was not breaking the law. This is simply another unfortunate case of the general public not understanding the true meaning of the Establishment Clause: "Congress shall make no law respecting an establishment of religion." What is even more relevant in this case is the Free Exercise Clause, which states that Congress shall not prohibit the free exercise of religion, including in any public arena. As we described in more detail in Chapter 5, both of these aspects of the First Amendment protect freedom of religion. In most cases, sacred songs may be sung if they are included among secular songs or songs of other faiths. The famous court case *Crockett v. Sorenson* (U.S. District Court, W. D. Va. 1983) declares this:

> The First Amendment was never intended to insulate our public institutions from any mention of God, the Bible or religion. When such insulation occurs, another religion, such as secular humanism, is effectively established.

Many court cases have upheld the right for sacred songs to be sung in public schools, as long as secular songs are also included in the program.

Mathew Staver of Liberty Counsel details many cases on this subject in his book *Eternal Vigilance*.[18] One Supreme Court Justice explained it like this: "music without sacred music, architecture minus the Cathedral, or painting without the Scriptural themes would be eccentric and incomplete, even from a secular view."[19] In the case *Doe v. Duncanville Independent School District*, the court found that 60–75% of serious choral music is based on sacred themes or text.[20] The ruling said this:

> Given the dominance of religious music in this field, [the school district] can hardly be presumed to be advancing or endorsing religion by allowing its choirs to sing a religious theme song . . . Indeed, to forbid , [the school district] from having a theme song that is religious would force, [the school district] to disqualify the majority of appropriate choral music simply because it is religious. Within the world of choral music, such a restriction would require hostility, not neutrality, toward religion.

Because our culture has such strong historical Judeo-Christian roots, many songs will have Christian references. Staver also uses the guidelines from the Sioux Falls School District in

[18] Mathew Staver, *Eternal Vigilance*, pp. 156–165
[19] *McCollum*, 333 U.S. at 236 (Jackson, J. concurring)
[20] *Doe v. Duncanville Independent School District*, 70 F.3d 402 (5th Cir. 1995)

South Dakota as an illustration of "permissibility for the use of symbols, music, art, drama, and literature within the public school system." The reason he uses this policy as an example is because it has been court tested, meaning it has survived one or more legal battles and won.[21] The Sioux Falls policy that was upheld says this about sacred music:

> Music, art, literature, and drama having religious themes or bases are permitted as part of the curriculum for school-sponsored activities and programs if presented in a prudent and objective manner and as a traditional part of the cultural and religious heritage of the particular holiday.

These rulings are the tip of the iceberg in terms of court rulings that uphold a teacher's right to include Christian references in the area of music and the arts. We see that the choir teacher in Oregon was on firm legal ground by including Wesley's hymn in the program. We hope that the teachers and administrators realize that they did not break the law.

May the words to Wesley's hymn ring for many years to come in public school choirs around the country.

WHAT ABOUT REFERENCES TO OTHER RELIGIONS?

A common argument promoting a complete separation of church and state goes something like this. If we incorporate Christian references into schools, won't we then be required to incorporate other religions? Don't we want to protect our students from deception by members of other religions? There are several important points to make regarding these questions.

First, *all* proselytizing is illegal by teachers during school hours, whether by Christians, Jews, Muslims, witches, Eastern religions, or the local atheist society. We are advocating that Christianity should be included in curriculum and classroom activities in an appropriate way as directed by content standards. When we talk about allowing sacred Christian songs in school

---

[21] *Florey v. Sioux Falls School District*, 49–5, 619 F.2d 1311, 1319 (8th Cir. 1980), cert. denied, 449 U.S. 987 (1980)

concerts, for example, it is not for the purpose of evangelizing. Sacred Christian songs are appropriate in a concert because 60–75% of all choir music is sacred in nature, as the courts rightly pointed out (see section above). Because we live in a country with a rich Christian heritage and that was clearly founded on numerous Christian principles, mention of Christianity will also naturally be appropriate in many more places within curricular areas than any other religions. To back this up, simply view your state's content standards. What is ironic is that much of our Christian heritage has been *extracted* from our schools even though the standards say it really ought to be there!

Second, if we ditch all religious references in schools, we end up with a religion of secularism, as the courts have repeatedly pointed out. Most Christians would rather have the fair and appropriate inclusion of various religions than have a religion of secularism dominate the schools. When we write a Prepare the Way post about our Christian heritage or sacred Christian music in schools, we inevitably get the Facebook response that says something like this: "So you want to include Christianity in schools. Then I assume it's okay with you if we also start reciting Muslim prayers during Ramadan or memorizing parts of the Koran?" My answer to this is as follows: if you are teaching a class on world religions and you are teaching on Islam, it would be appropriate to include how Muslims celebrate Ramadan. However, you would never need to recite Muslim prayers or memorize any parts of the Koran. Furthermore, if you are teaching U.S. history, reciting Muslim prayers is totally off topic. However, objectively learning about the Christian roots of America is totally appropriate and in fact needed to understand our history. We are not advocating that all students recite the Nicene Creed in American history class, and naturally we are not advocating they recite Muslim prayers either. Generally, I would rather have teachers use primary source documents when religious topics arise (when appropriate for content standards) and let students draw their own conclusions. Primary source documents are a much more interesting way to study history and many subjects. We simply need to keep in mind that the purpose of using primary source documents is to study history, not to make converts. Again, because of the deep Christian roots of our nation, there will be many more primary source documents with Christian reference that are appropriate according to educational standards. These cases take wisdom. When questions arise, we encourage parents, teachers and students to consult the free Christian legal firms listed in Chapter 11.

RIGHTS OF EXTRACURRICULAR GROUPS

There are many Christian groups that are active in the public school system and doing great work in maintaining a Christian presence on campuses across the country. Moms in Prayer, Child Evangelism Fellowship, Young Life, Fellowship of Christian Athletes, and others are all allowed by law to meet on public school property. Our federal courts have declared: "[R]eligiously-oriented student activities must be allowed under the same terms and conditions as other extracurricular activities."[22] In the case *Brown v. Gilmore (2001)*, the courts clarified this right:

> Religion Clauses must not be interpreted with a view that religion be suppressed in the public arenas in favor of secularism . . . The Constitution "does not require total separation of Church and State." . . . Not only is the government permitted to accommodate religion without violating the Establishment Clause, at times it is required to do so.

The courts have been very clear about equal access to public school facilities. If something of a secular nature is allowed to happen on campus, then the similar religious activity must be allowed. Otherwise the school will be guilty of "viewpoint discrimination," which is illegal. However, there are certain restrictions that groups should be aware of. For example, if a group of Christians wanted to organize an event or meeting on campus during regular school hours, it would need to be completely student led and non-disruptive. A Bible study could be organized and run by students during a lunch hour, or an evangelism outreach could be set up during non-instructional time during the school day. In comparison, after-school activities are much less restrictive; there is much more freedom for Christian groups when school is not

---

[22] U.S. Federal Court, *Prince v. Jacoby*, 2002

actually in session. For example, if a school allows any secular group to use their facilities during non-instructional time, than they have to allow Christian groups the same privilege.

It is important for Christians to realize that the rights we now enjoy are being consistently attacked. If we would like to be able to continue to have the right to a Christian presence on school campuses, then we ought to be involved and vigilant about protecting those rights. For example, Good News Clubs (organized by Child Evangelism Fellowship) have been badgered with lawsuits for years. Finally, the U.S. Supreme Court delivered a decisive ruling, protecting CEF's right to meet in public schools. The magazine *Christianity Today* commented on the case:

> The U.S. Supreme Court decision upholding the right of religious groups to meet in public school buildings will establish broad protections for free speech . . . the Court ruled in *Good News Club* v. *Milford Central School* that religious clubs cannot be prevented from meeting at public schools after hours if other private groups are allowed to meet during that time. In a 6–3 opinion written by Justice Clarence Thomas, the Court said excluding a club because of its religious viewpoint violates the First Amendment.[23]

There are now thousands of Good News Clubs meeting in public schools all across the nation, because Christians were willing to stand in the face of opposition. The courts also ruled, shortly after the above-mentioned case, that not only can Good News Clubs meet on public school campuses, but that teachers may lead them. Though public school staff are prohibited from openly proselytizing students during the school day, they are completely free to encourage students to become Christians in an after-school Christian club, after the bell rings. As mentioned earlier, we started a Good News Club at my elementary school and I was legally able to share the gospel, read and hand out Bibles, pray with my students, and help lead them to a saving knowledge of Jesus Christ—all on our public school campus.

If you are involved in planning Christian events with a church or ministry, it is helpful to understand your rights in

---

[23] www.ChristianityToday.com, "Supreme Court: Court Ruling is Good News for Equal Access," August 6, 2001

general public settings as well. You want to make sure you are on firm legal ground when choosing a venue or putting up flyers. The courts have established that there are three types of public forums, each with varying degrees of restrictions on freedom of speech: Public Forum, Limited Public Forum, and Nonpublic Forum. There are few restrictions for religious expression in a traditional Public Forum, such as parks, streets, and sidewalks. The second category, a Limited Public Forum, would include any government buildings that have been opened for use by the public. This could include public schools, libraries, public arenas, and other public facilities. There are more restrictions in these places, but the general law is that religious speakers and activities must receive equal access to the facilities on the same terms as non-religious speakers and events. Nonpublic Forums include airports, metros, rails, and bus stations. These venues are more restrictive, but must not allow viewpoint discrimination.[24]

Christians are free to read Scripture and evangelize in public parks and on public streets. This freedom covers speech and written material (including flyers and signs). In public schools, or other public facilities, Christian groups have to be allowed the same equal access to the facility that secular groups are allowed.

A Biblical and Historical Perspective on the Concept of Rights

I have heard countless Christians say that "one of the greatest lies one can believe is that we even have rights." Let's make an important distinction between *rights before God* and *rights in relation to other humans*. It is only by God's grace (because Jesus Christ shed His blood for us) that we can have any relationship at all with Him, so in that sense we do not have intrinsic "rights" before God. However, the Bible does outline appropriate and inappropriate behavior toward other human beings. When we clarify "right" living among humans, we are essentially defining "rights." Do we have a Biblically-based moral right that says people cannot walk into our homes and take what they want? Yes, the Bible outlines

---

[21] Mathew Staver, *Eternal Vigilance*

in the Ten Commandments that we should not steal from one another. Do we have a Biblically-based moral right that prevents one person shooting another in the midst of an argument? Yes, the Bible says not to murder. There are countless guidelines presented in the Bible for appropriate treatment of other human beings. When founding documents discuss our rights, they are not referring to rights before God, but our God-given rights as citizens of planet Earth.

Let's clarify how the Founders viewed these human rights. First, and very importantly, the Founders believed that our rights come from *God*. As the Declaration of Independence famously states: "We hold these truths to be self-evident, that all men are created equal, that they are endowed by their Creator with certain unalienable Rights, that among these are Life, Liberty and the pursuit of Happiness." This is perhaps the most important feature of our government and is the exact point that separated us from all other countries at the time of our founding. All other governments at the time of the Declaration believed that their citizens' rights came from those running the government. In the case of the monarchies, the king or queen had ultimate power. They generally believed that God had bestowed on them a divine right to rule. Hence, according to those governments, the rights of the people came from the government. The United States was the first government "of the people, by the people, and for the people."[25] It was the first government whose very founding documents stated that every human being has intrinsic value and possesses God-given rights to "Life, Liberty and the pursuit of Happiness."

One can trace the radical (for the time) concept that our rights come directly from God to the earliest founding documents of our country. Founding documents often refer to these rights as "natural rights." In *The Rights of the Colonists*, Samuel Adams refers to our natural rights and the fact that it is the chief aim of civil government to protect those natural rights:

> In short, it is the greatest absurdity to suppose it in the power of one, or any number of men, at the entering into society, to renounce their essential natural rights, or the means of preserving those rights; when the grand end of civil government, from

---

[25] Abraham Lincoln, *Gettysburg Address*, 1863

the very nature of its institution, is for the support, protection, and defence of those very rights; the principal of which, as is before observed, are Life, Liberty, and Property.[26]

Adams makes the point that it is unreasonable to expect citizens to renounce their natural rights when entering into a society, when it is the job of the society (government) to protect those natural rights. He concludes that this is illogical by the very definition of our form of government.

Second, the Founders believed that the moral foundation of our country and our concept of government was rooted in Christianity. Therefore, our rights (in terms of appropriate treatment of human beings) should be learned from the Bible. To quote *The Rights of the Colonists* again:

> These [rights] may be best understood by reading and carefully studying the institutes of the great Law Giver and Head of the Christian Church, which are to be found clearly written and promulgated in the New Testament.

From the "Constitution State" of Connecticut, we see the roots of this same principle in the *Fundamental Orders of Connecticut* (1639), a precursor to our federal Constitution:

> [W]ell knowing when a people are gathered together, the word of God requires that to maintain the peace and union of such a people, there should be an orderly and decent government established according to God.

According to this statement, our society should base its moral standards on the "word of God," and reflect an "orderly and decent government" by God's standards. The rights that the Founders wrote about were not given by a vague concept of God. The Founders were clearly talking about rights based on Biblical teaching and Christian morality. John Quincy Adams, son of John Adams, referred to Christian principles as the foundation of government:

> [T]he Declaration of Independence first organized the social compact on the foundation of the Redeemer's mission upon earth. . . . [and] laid the cornerstone of human government upon the first precepts of Christianity.

---

[26] Samuel Adams, *The Rights of the Colonists*, 1772

As noted before, in William Penn's *Frame of Government* of Pennsylvania (1682), Penn clarifies the two main goals of government from a Biblical perspective, to punish evil-doers and protect citizens (referencing Romans 13):

> Let every soul be subject to the higher powers; for there is no power but of *God* . . . This settles the divine right of government beyond exception, and that for two ends: first, to terrify evildoers; secondly, to cherish those that do well; which gives government a life beyond corruption and makes it as durable in the world, as good men shall be. So that government seems to me a part of religion itself, a thing sacred in its institution and end.

Penn also made the connection that government is intertwined with religion at some level, because government will always reflect someone's morality. It is just a matter of which religion is reflected—secular humanist, Christian, Eastern, etc. In the case of the Founders, the laws were intentionally aligned with a Christian worldview.

Third, the Founders felt that it was the duty of government to protect these God-ordained rights of individuals and if the government was not passing laws in accordance with that aim, it was the duty of the people to pursue a new form of government that would protect them. The preamble of the Declaration of Independence clearly declares:

> When in the Course of human events, it becomes necessary for one people to dissolve the political bands which have connected them with another, and to assume among the powers of the earth, the separate and equal station to which the Laws of Nature and of Nature's God entitle them . . .

People frequently question what was meant by the "Laws of Nature" and of "Nature's God." Some revisionists of history would have us believe that these are mere secular phrases and not Biblical ideas. This is simply false. The famous English lawyer and jurist William Blackstone was hugely influential on Thomas Jefferson and the framing of our way of government. Blackstone defines these phrases as follows:

> Thus when the Supreme Being formed the universe, and created matter out of nothing, he impressed certain principles

upon that matter, from which it can never depart, and without which it would cease to be . . . This *law of nature*, being coeval [coexistent] with mankind and dictated by God himself, is of course superior in obligation to any other . . . Upon these two foundations, the law of nature and the law of revelation [from Scripture], depend all human laws; that is to say, no human laws should be suffered [permitted] to contradict these.[27]

Jefferson, a lawyer himself, said that lawyers cite Blackstone like Muslims quote the Koran.[28] Blackstone was defining the secular terms for what theologians teach from a Biblical worldview in regards to General Revelation and Specific Revelation. His point is that no human laws should ever contradict any laws from God. This point is precisely what was meant in the preamble of our Declaration and it was held consistently throughout the forming of our government. For example, John Jay, the original Chief Justice of the U.S. Supreme Court, said this,

The Bible is the best of all books, for it is the word of God and teaches us the way to be happy in this world and in the next. Continue therefore to read it and to regulate your life by its precepts.[29]

In addition, President John Adams said this,

Suppose a nation in some distant region should take the Bible for their only law book and every member should regulate his conduct by the precepts there exhibited . . . What a Eutopia, what a Paradise would this region be. I have examined all [religions] . . . and the result is that the Bible is the best Book in the world. It contains more of my little philosophy than all the libraries I have seen.[30]

Due to the long history of abuse of power by human governments, particularly by rulers who assumed almost God-like power over their subjects, the Founders were radical and unbending in their articulation that all citizens have God-given rights that their

---

27 Sir Williams Blackstone, *Of The Nature of Laws in General*, Commentaries, 1753

28 David Barton, *Original Intent*, 2013

29 Dreisbach and Hall, *Faith and the Founders of the American Republic*, Oxford University Press, 2014, p. 149

30 Stephen McDowell, *Building Godly Nations*, Providence Foundation, 2004, p. 69

government is entrusted to protect. Their conclusion was that they ought not to tolerate a tyrannical government that abuses its citizens by denying them the rights that they have been given by God.

To summarize, we do not have rights before God, but God gives us moral direction through the Bible that clarifies the rights we have between human beings. The point is that our rights are given to us by God. The American Founders voiced this radical (for their time) idea that all human beings have rights given to them by God, and that the government's job is to protect those God-given rights. These God-given rights clarify how we should be treated by others, including by our government. When government places itself above God, or removes accountability to Him, then it will tend towards corruption and abuse. The Founders understood this danger, and it is why they formed a constitutional republic, "under God"; this form of government was intended to protect American citizens from a future government that rejected God-ordained rights for its people.

GUARDING OUR RIGHTS THROUGH POLITICAL ACTION . . . AT WHAT LEVEL ARE YOU CALLED?

We are all called to political action at some level. For some, it may mean simply casting your vote and paying your taxes (per Jesus's teaching). Some Christians, though, may have a special gifting in the political arena; if this rings true for you, do not be afraid to join others in pursuing that calling. As President James Garfield stated:

> If the next centennial does not find us a great nation . . . it will be because those who represent the enterprise, the culture, and the morality of the nation do not aid in controlling the political forces.[31]

If the political arena is your calling, you will be much more effective if you join with others who are trying to make an influence in this sphere. Because politics has at times caused such division in the Church, some pastors and churches shy away from it and may even discourage political involvement. This is un-Biblical.

---

[31] James A. Garfield, *A Century of Congress*, July, 1877

Theologian and evangelical Biblical scholar Wayne Grudem writes a compelling Biblical argument that all Christians are called to give "significant" influence in the political sphere. Grudem describes this view in his outstanding book *Politics According to the Bible*:

> The "significant influence" view says that Christians *should* seek to influence civil government according to God's moral standards and God's purposes for government as revealed in the Bible (when rightly understood). But while Christians exercise this influence, they must simultaneously insist on protecting freedom of religion for all citizens. In addition, "significant influence" does not mean angry, belligerent, intolerant, judgmental, red-faced, and hate-filled influence, but rather winsome, kind, thoughtful, loving, persuasive influence that is suitable to each circumstance and that always protects the other person's right to disagree, but that is also uncompromising about the truthfulness and moral goodness of the teachings of God's Word.[32]

It is true that politics cannot remotely save us in the same way that Jesus Christ can save us from the problem of sin. It is also true that we cannot somehow politically force people to become Christians or agree with Christian morality. However, we ought to be careful not to throw the baby out with the bath water. Many Christians say that we should simply focus on sharing the gospel. Yes, we should absolutely do that. What they sometimes seem to forget is that our freedom to share the gospel is under massive attack. Christians must realize that laws and judicial rulings vastly influence our ability to both share the gospel and exercise our freedom of religion, which are God-given rights worth fighting for.

The political sphere has great power over our public educational system. Politics influences curriculum choices, which in turn significantly sway the worldview of our students. We would be naïve to believe there are not strong political forces out there that are fighting a Christian worldview and trying to negatively "spin" Christianity, or even to filter Christianity out of our schools and society completely.

Politics also impacts the freedom that Christian groups have on campuses. In recent years, there have been many rulings that

[32] Wayne Grudem, *Politics According to the Bible: A Comprehensive Resource for Understanding Modern Political Issues in Light of Scripture*, Zondervan, 2010, p.55

have hindered Christian groups from meeting on campus due to some very active political agendas. Meanwhile, many Christians have been politically asleep, letting these Christian groups get thrown under the bus, so to speak. For example, people we talk to are frequently not aware that campus Christian groups, such as InterVarsity Christian Fellowship, are increasingly banned on university campuses across the nation.[33] InterVarsity was expelled from the California State college system recently because they would not allow a non-Christian on their leadership board. Can you imagine the leading campus atheist as president of the local college Christian club? Nonsensical? Yes, yet that is the direction of the political flow in California.

Christian lawyers and legal groups are continually fighting to protect Child Evangelism Fellowship (CEF), Young Life, Campus Crusade (CRU), Fellowship of Christian Athletes, and every Christian group that aims to be salt and light in our educational system. Who will take action to defend these groups and help their work continue? Why are CEF's Good News Clubs still allowed to meet in elementary schools across the nation? Because some Christians were brave enough to defend the clubs' rights all the way to the Supreme Court, as noted above. Was this an easy road for these Christians? No. Is there eternal fruit? Yes.

Our educational system is greatly influenced by political agendas, and many Christians are called to be involved at the political level in order to protect our religious freedoms. The famous preacher Charles Finney, who was born shortly after the American Constitution was ratified, exhorted Christians to be involved in politics:

> Politics are part of religion in such a country as this and Christians must do their duty to the country as a part of their duty to God. It seems sometimes as if the foundations of the nation are becoming rotten and Christians seem to act as if they think God does not see what they do in politics. But I tell you He does see it, and He will bless or curse this nation, according to the course they [Christians] take [in politics].[34]

---

[33] https://intervarsity.org/page/campus-challenges
[34] Rev. Charles Finney quoted by Peter Marshall and David Manuel, *From Sea to Shining Sea*, Revell, 1986

We must realize that *all* laws are based on *someone's* morality. It just depends on *which someone* wins the political fight in a particular area. When we pass a law that says murder is wrong, it is because we are making a moral conclusion that murder is wrong. There is a notion out there that if Christians try to pass laws in line with Judeo-Christian values, that we are somehow being judgmental. The saying "you can't legislate morality" is not only a popular bumper sticker; it permeates the mentality of many Americans, including Christians. This saying is nonsensical, because all laws are based on some moral code. The whole point of laws is to legislate morality. It is only a matter of *whose* morality is being legislated.

For hundreds of years, our nation's moral code and subsequent laws were based on a Judeo-Christian ethical foundation. Throughout our history, we have chosen which moral rules should be made into laws and which should be left up to individuals or organizations. For example, our government will legislate moral codes in the area of murder (except for unborn babies) or stealing. Government officials have rightly decided to not legislate moral codes about swearing or blasphemy. Does the Bible say not to swear and definitely not to blaspheme God? Yes, but do we throw people in jail for it? No. The government has rightly relegated these types of sins or immorality to the Church, family, and individuals to deal with as they see fit. There is a Biblical concept known as Sphere Sovereignty, which shows that God has ordained certain institutions (Church, state, family, individual) to have their own independent authority under Him. There is a constant tension between what to legislate in the governmental sphere and what to relegate, so we need to elect officials who have the wisdom to navigate that tension well.

So how do we take action in the political arena? First, we are called to pray for everyone in office or in any position of power in our culture. The apostle Paul exhorts us in First Timothy 2:1–2, "I exhort, therefore, that first of all, supplications, prayers, intercessions, and giving of thanks, be made for all men, for kings, and for all that are in authority, that we may lead a quiet and peaceable life in all godliness and honesty." This concept was not new to Christians, either. When Judah was carried off to Babylon, God commanded them to pray for the Babylonian government. Consider Jeremiah 29:7, "Seek the welfare of the city where I have sent you into exile, and pray to the LORD on its behalf; for in its welfare you will have welfare." God was speaking to the remnant left in Babylon during their seventy-year exile. If they were told to pray for a government which was openly and completely hostile towards the Lord, how much more should we be concerned with praying for our nation?

Second, at the very basic level, Christians should take voting seriously. As President Teddy Roosevelt said, "The people who say they have not time to attend to politics are simply saying they are unfit to live in a free community." Yet in the 2010 election, 30 million Evangelical Christians did *not* vote. By doing so, David Crowe of Restore America poignantly states, "Christians are allowing an ungodly minority to disassemble our religious freedoms, erode our ability to share the gospel, and rewrite our history and laws."[35] In 1781, Samuel Adams exhorted Americans:

> Let each citizen remember at the moment he is offering his VOTE . . . that he is executing one of the most solemn trusts in human society for which he is accountable to God and his Country.

We must realize that all laws are based on someone's morality, and it is logical for Christians to desire that laws in our nation line up with a Judeo-Christian moral system. How do we do that? We make an effort to influence our government and to elect politicians who will take a stand for laws that are in alignment with Biblical principles. Christians have recognized this for years; it is mainly in recent years that Christians have let their freedom to vote fade in importance. Noah Webster said (1832):

> When you become entitled to exercise the right of voting for public officers, let it be impressed on your mind that God *commands* you to choose for rulers *just* men who will rule in the fear of God. The preservation of a republican government depends on the faithful discharge of this duty. [emphasis added]

John Jay, Chief Justice of the U.S. Supreme Court, said in 1816, "Providence has given our people the choice of their rulers, and it is the duty, as well as privilege and interest of a Christian nation to select and prefer Christians for their rulers . . ." If your children are

---

[35] www.RestoreAmerica.org

under 18, you can still go through the ballot with them and discuss key issues.

Third, we can encourage our pastors and church leaders to be aware of the political arena and to take appropriate action to protect our religious freedoms. Many pastors have been misinformed that their church could lose its 501c3 tax-exempt status if they speak out about or become involved in political issues. In reality, pastors have many more freedoms than they think when it comes to sharing about political issues from the pulpit. Here is a summary of what pastors can and cannot do.

Rights of Pastors and Churches (from Mathew Staver of Liberty Counsel)[36]

	Churches, 501(c)3s	*Pastor/Ministry Leader*
Endorsing/Opposing Political Candidates	No	Yes
Introduce Political Candidates at Church	Yes	Yes
Voter Registration Drives (non-partisan)	Yes	Yes
Discuss Viewpoints of Candidates	Yes	Yes
Discuss Viewpoints from a Biblical Worldview	Yes	Yes
Support/Oppose Judicial Appointments	Yes	Yes
Support/Oppose Any Legislation	Yes	Yes
Preach Sermons on Social Activism	Yes	Yes
Petition Drives to Support/Oppose Legislation	Yes	Yes
Lobby Candidates to Support/ Oppose Bills	Yes*	Yes

---

[36] Mathew Staver, "Civic Guidelines for Pastors and Churches," www.LC.org

Fourth, we should increase awareness of judicial activism. Many of the decisions in the past fifty years that have eroded a Christian presence from public schools (prayer in schools, Ten Commandments, etc) have originated from judges. Granted, these judges were put in place by elected officials (another reason to vote!). However, we can still take action once they are in office and, believe it or not, we can actually take actions to impeach judges. This idea has collected dust somewhat in recent years, but if it is revived, we could raise awareness of the issues at hand. Get educated by reading David Barton's book, *Restraining Judicial Activism*, or Phyllis Schlafly's *The Supremacists: The Tyranny of Judges and How to Stop It*. We can become informed about which judges are abusing their constitutional power, start a grassroots effort to educate other citizens, build a coalition of concerned citizens, and contact our representatives to inform and encourage them to impeach activist judges.

Fifth, we can exercise our voice in the community. Many people do not realize the powerful influence of simply writing their representatives and senators about key issues. We can also write editorials to the local newspapers. As Christians, we should be influencing these issues from a Biblical worldview and exhorting others to do the same. As the U.S. Supreme Court ruled in 1972 in *Police Department v. Mosley*,

> Above all else, the First Amendment means that the government has no power to restrict expression because of its message, its ideas, its subject matter or its content . . . The essence of this forbidden censorship is content control.

This is another reminder of the phrase we mentioned earlier: *silence equals consent*. It would be wise to remember that when we are silent, that is actually taking action, but the wrong kind.

CONCLUSIONS

Knowing and exercising your rights is crucial to navigating the public school system effectively. In this chapter we have helped to clarify the rights of students, parents, staff, and extracurricular groups. Keep your rights on your radar, so that you can be empowered to use them. Remember: as you exercise your rights, speak the truth in love and be good ambassadors for Christ. Although we do not have rights before God, God gives us rights in relation to other humans. Our Founding Fathers referred to many of these rights as they declared their independence from Great Britain. Some Christian leaders have advised that we should not be overly concerned about our rights in public settings and have ceased fighting to protect them. However, this will lead to the silencing of Christians and will hinder the sharing of the gospel. It will also potentially cause more Christians to stumble in their faith. In a country where God has given us the ability to influence how freely the gospel can be shared, we would be poor stewards of these God-given rights if we were to simply allow them to be taken away. We encourage you to participate in protecting your religious freedoms. It is true that, at some point, it is possible that despite our best efforts, we will lose those rights to share the gospel freely. But until that time, we should be aware of the battle and be active in preserving our rights in the public arena.

CHAPTER 7

CHART YOUR COURSE: PREPARE FOR CURRICULUM ISSUES—HISTORY/SOCIAL STUDIES

[T]he American people should know the history and nature of the civil institutions of their Christian republic . . . and thus be qualified to discharge with fidelity and conscientiousness all the duties of an American citizen![1]

—Dr. Benjamin F. Morris, 1864

In many ways, sending your children into the public school system is like standing before a picture of a sailboat sailing in the beautiful blue Caribbean. Who wouldn't want to be sailing in those sparkling seas? But while the warm turquoise waters might look like smooth sailing, anyone who has sailed around the Caribbean islands will tell you that it is not as easy as it looks. There are many hidden hazards: challenging currents, winds, shoals, sudden changes in weather. Public schools are similar in many ways. When you see your child greeted by smiling teachers and administrators, you can easily get the feeling that your child's experience in that school will be simply wonderful. You might be dazzled by organized and talented teachers and an expensive curriculum. Many schools are indeed impressive. And I certainly agree: there are

---

[1] Benjamin F. Morris, *The Christian Life and Character of the Civil Institutions of the United States*, 1864

many wonderful teachers and administrators in public schools. However, as Christians navigate the waters of our American public school system, they frequently discover challenges that they didn't expect. A casual observer on the shore will only see a beautiful day for sailing, while a boat might actually be navigating through the shallow waters of a coral reef, fighting strong trade winds or currents, or about to be threatened with a sudden storm. In the same way, a secular worldview is often woven throughout the public school system without parents' knowledge. As a result, many children end up feeling ashamed of a Biblical worldview, and their faith can get "blown off course" or even shipwrecked.

The old saying, "you can't always judge a book by its cover," applies to our public schools. I have found that most parents are not aware of serious curriculum issues that can compromise their children's faith in schools. Most parents of public school students cannot realistically sort through endless curriculum and homework assignments and find all of the places where a secular worldview is pushed. Given the fast pace of our culture, this would be an overwhelming task. A more reasonable approach is to do several things in an intentional and ongoing way.

First, teach your kids to exercise their worldview muscles. Teach them how to decipher a Biblical worldview and a secular worldview (as previous chapters have described) and encourage them to do their work with a discerning mind. Second, keep the lines of communication open and strong. Ask them regularly how their assignments are going and if they have noticed places that seem to be promoting a secular worldview. Create time and space for communication about these topics (in a casual and encouraging way). Third, *do* spend some time learning along with your children about the hot topic curriculum issues that most often have an anti-Christian agenda. These key curriculum issues will inevitably come up while navigating through the public school system, so it is wise to be prepared. Invest in some resources and books on these topics and make an effort to teach these topics to your children. We will summarize some of the key curriculum issues below; this will get you started. The major areas that we will examine are history/social studies, science, sex education, anti-bullying, holidays, literature, and Common Core. Though an anti-Christian worldview can occur anywhere, we have found that some of the most damage often happens in these areas or something related to them.

Curriculum Issue #1: History/Social Studies

History is frequently distorted in schools in three ways, all of which can negatively influence a child's faith.[2] We'll go into detail on how these areas are played out in schools, but the net effect of this revisionist history is that many Christians feel ashamed of their faith and non-believers become more hostile towards Christianity. First, there is frequently a *Biased Presentation* of Christianity, where the positive aspects of the religion are eliminated or downplayed and the negative things done in the name of Jesus are highlighted. Second, *Omission* of Christian references takes place. References to Christianity, God, or Jesus Christ are often edited out of primary source quotes and documents in textbooks, causing a revisionist secularization of our heritage. Thirdly, there is often a complete *Lack of Primary Source References* in textbooks and materials, especially when those primary sources include Christian references. These days, modern opinions are used more than original sources from the relevant time period. In this chapter, we will take a closer look at each of these aspects of revisionist history, how they can affect your student, and what resources you can access to correct the curriculum at home.

Historical Revisionism: Biased Presentation of Christianity

Curricula and textbooks used in public schools often focus on any negative influence that Christianity has had throughout history and minimize any positive role that it has played. Now, I want to be clear that I am *not* supportive of hiding bad things in history that have been done in the name of Christianity. I would simply like to see a more balanced view presented to students. We will

---

[2] Paul Vitz, *Censorship: Evidence of Bias in our Children's Textbooks*, Servant Books, 1986

take a quick quiz to highlight my point. What's the first thing that comes to mind from your public school education when you think of the Puritans? Most people immediately think of the Salem witch trials. This is a sad commentary on our public school system, because the Salem witch trials are a tiny blip when you consider the positive contributions the Puritans made to our government and society. Remember from Chapter 2 that it was the Puritans who championed the concept of education for all children! Yet this fact is frequently either downplayed or completely over-looked in public schools. The "Old Deluder Satan Law" radically transformed the value of education in our society. Because of the Puritan's Christian worldview where all children (boys *and* girls) should be educated to read the Bible, literacy rates skyrocketed. Recall that the law helped increase the literacy rate in the colonies to over 90% by the Revolutionary War. Prior to that time in the history of the known world, only select classes of people were educated, typically males of noble or wealthy origin. Yet sadly, in most schools today, more time is spent on the Salem witch trials when studying the Puritans than a vast array of other significant contributions that they made to our culture and nation.

When I was a 5th-grade teacher, one activity we did every year was a living history day called Colonial Day. All the teachers and students would dress up in Colonial era clothing and we would have stations with hands-on activities representing that time period. The day would begin by gathering the entire 5th grade, together with teachers and parents, to watch a play written by the students and directed by a teacher. It was somewhat of a tradition for one particular teacher to run the play each year. Almost every year, the topic happened to be the Salem witch trials. Over the course of several weeks, the students did in depth research on the Salem witch trials, wrote an original script, created props, costumes, and scenery. The project was time intensive and always well done. But every year, the moral of the story was the same. Christianity is dangerous. When Christians influence our government and society, people get hurt and die. Year after year, the Puritans as a whole were portrayed as mean-spirited tyrants.

If those students were asked what they remembered about the Puritans, I am sure it would be the Salem witch trials. The truth is, their classroom learning was heavily weighted towards this unfortunate event. There was little in the textbooks or school curriculum that discussed the vast array of other significant contributions that the Puritans made to our culture and nation. Now, I am not saying that we should hide injustices done in the name of Christianity. Nineteen people died in the Salem witch trials, and that was tragic. However, the Puritans made many positive contributions to our nation that are rarely addressed. Remember, it was the Puritans who taught that everyone should be educated, regardless of race and gender, and it was the Puritans who were responsible for spearheading public education in the first place!

In addition to the undue amount of time and focus on the Salem witch trials, Colonial Day also included a School House station, where the teacher would be brutally strict, threatening students with a stick while waiving around a Bible. The kids of course got a kick out his behavior, but suffice it to say, Christians were once again portrayed in a very negative and condescending way. When I asked to host the School House station one year, hoping to give a more accurate portrayal of schoolhouse life, the teacher in charge refused. Church and faith were incredibly important parts of Colonial life, yet throughout our school's Colonial Day, there was no station that portrayed Christianity in a fair light! There was even a Tavern Life station, but of course, no Church station. While they were brainstorming ideas for the Tavern station, it was suggested that kids come in with pennies to pay for drinks (grossly distorting what actually happened in taverns of the time). The teacher running that station, posing as the bartender, enthusiastically replied, "Yeah, I'll say to the kids, *what's your poison?*" Sadly, this is more accepted in our culture than mentioning the Ten Commandments.

I think examples like overemphasizing the Salem witch trials and other negative portrayals of Christians (while leaving out positive contributions made by Christians) can leave students feeling ashamed of their faith. However, if you were a parent with a student involved in Colonial Day, and you stayed current and involved in classroom activities, you would have an opportunity to address these issues with your student either before or during the event. You could better protect your student and provide a more balanced view of our Christian heritage. Many parents lose these opportunities because they do not keep up to date about activities and curriculum, and the additive effect of classroom experiences with a bias against a Christian worldview can slowly erode their kids' faith. If you are one of the estimated 600,000 conservative Christian teachers in public schools,[3] you have a unique opportunity to present primary source documents that balance out the mostly negative portrayal of Christianity in our nation's history.

Another example of *Biased Presentation* is when students study what motivated the Founding Fathers to declare their independence from Britain. What was the major injustice that caused the United States to declare our independence? Most Americans today would say, "Taxation without representation." In other words, it's all about the money. This again is a gross misrepresentation of what motivated the Founders. They clearly and definitively explained the reasons for the separation in the Declaration of Independence. Of the 27 reasons listed in the Declaration, only *one* had to do with money! The vast majority of the reasons were moral grievances linked to the concept of "the Laws of Nature and of Nature's God" and the fact that people "are endowed by their Creator with certain unalienable Rights, that among these are Life, Liberty and the pursuit of Happiness." Many of the Founding Fathers were influenced by their faith in God and had examined their actions in light of Biblical morality. Jefferson stated that the overarching reasons for independence were violations of God-given rights to life, liberty (freedom), and the pursuit of happiness (including, predominantly, a right to own property). These God-given rights were so obvious to the Founders that they called them "self-evident." This is a key concept that is downplayed or neglected altogether in the public educational system.

The consequence of *Biased Presentation* is to give students a predominantly negative view towards Christianity.

Historical Revisionism: Omission in Practice

Historical revisionism in the form of omission occurs when authors leave out references to God, Jesus, or Christianity in quotes. This practice happens most often when textbooks include only the secular portion of primary sources, leaving out any portion that

---

[3] Gateways to a Better Education, www.gtbe.org

mentions God. The content of approved public school textbooks must pass through special committees set up by publishing companies before they are accepted. These committees handle what content is covered and also deal with any issue which they think might be "insensitive" or not politically correct. In effect, they can become committees that specialize in making sure textbooks are politically correct. When words such as "Christian, Jesus Christ, God, Divine, Almighty, Bible, Providence, etc." are seen in quotes, many times they are removed for fear of offending someone.

Here are some examples from 5th-grade textbooks used by hundreds of thousands of students across America.[4] The first example addresses the motivation of the Pilgrims to settle in America. The most important primary source document dealing with this is the Mayflower Compact, which states the purpose and goals of the Pilgrims' first colony in North America:

> In the name of God. Amen. We, whose names are under-written . . . Having undertaken, for the glory of God, and advancements of the Christian faith . . . do by these presents, solemnly and mutually, in the presence of God, and one another, covenant and combine ourselves together into a civil body politic; for our better ordering, and preservation and furtherance of the ends aforesaid;

So the Pilgrims themselves said that their overarching purpose in combining themselves "into a civil body politick" was to "glorify God" and for the "advancement of the Christian faith." Yet most textbooks omit the references to God, Christianity, and the spreading of the Gospel. The textbook I had to use in my classroom *paraphrased* the above passage this way:

> In the Mayflower Compact the colonists agreed to "combine ourselves together" and create and obey "just and equal laws."[5]

All references to God, glorifying God, and advancing the Christian faith were left out, and instead the quote was secularized. The focus was on the secular versus the Divine. This is a classic example of the kind of omission that happens all too frequently in

---

[4] *A New Nation*, McGraw-Hill School Division, 2000 and *United States*, McGraw-Hill School Division, 1999

[5] *A New Nation*, p. 176

textbooks across our nation. The end result is that our history is secularized.

The next example of omission from the same 5th-grade textbook is how the Declaration of Independence is paraphrased. The textbook breaks the Declaration of Independence into several different sections. Let's look at the first actual primary source section of the Declaration:

> We, therefore, the Representatives of the United States of America, in General Congress Assembled, appealing to the Supreme judge of the world . . .

The paraphrase presented in history textbooks across America reads as follows:

> In the name of the American people, we members of the Continental Congress . . . [6]

McGraw-Hill decided that the phrase "appealing to the Supreme judge of the world" was unnecessary or extraneous. What is ironic about this decision is that every one of the 56 signers of the Declaration knew that they were signing their death sentence not only for themselves, but also for their families, if they lost the resulting war with Great Britain. They knew that Britain was the world's military superpower at the time and could easily crush them. They knew that the ragtag Colonial army was no match for Great Britain's professional army. You bet the Founders were indeed "appealing to the Supreme judge of the world" to intercede on their behalf, because they knew that without His intercession, they would be destroyed! If you look back at other primary source historical writings of the time, they confirm the Founders' reliance on God in those harrowing times.

Here is one more comparison of how the Declaration of Independence actually reads, and how McGraw-Hill paraphrases (i.e., distorts) it. The primary source excerpt from the Declaration states:

> And for the support of this Declaration, with a firm reliance on the protection of divine Providence, we mutually pledge to each other . . .

---

[6] *United States*, McGraw-Hill School Division, 1999, p. R21

The public school history textbook paraphrases it as follows:

> To support this Declaration of Independence, we promise to each other . . . [7]

Once again we see that McGraw-Hill decided along the way that "with a firm reliance on the protection of divine Providence" was unnecessary in capturing the true heart of the phrase from the actual Declaration. As stated above, the Founders made it clear in their historical writings that without a firm reliance on the protection of God, they would not have gone forward with this revolutionary Declaration of Independence. Publishers of public school textbooks are rewriting our history through omission of key Christian ideals, and the result is that our children's view of history—and thus their thinking—is becoming increasingly secularized.

HISTORICAL REVISIONISM: LACK OF PRIMARY SOURCE REFERENCES

Next, we will investigate some examples of how textbooks and authors sometimes simply choose not to cite any primary sources at all in their discussions of our history. In fact, this was a key issue in me pursuing the federal court case against my school district. The final straw that broke the camel's back was when my principal prevented me from presenting my students with various primary source documents of our nation's history because of the supposed "separation of church and state." It is important to understand that the California Framework Standards, which describe what teachers should be teaching, include a whole section on using primary sources. As previously touched on, here's the actual text from the California content standards published by the California Department of Education:

> Teachers of history at all grade levels have recently begun to encourage their students not just to study history but to investigate it, in much the same way that professional historians engage in research into the past. Teachers attest that this is one of the

---

[7] Ibid.

best ways to make history exciting for their students, and also to increase students' retention and understanding of the material.

Fundamental to this process are primary sources, which lie as much at the heart of history as experiments lie at the heart of science. Students of history should be given opportunities to read and analyze primary sources, to wrestle with their meanings, and to attempt to interpret them and place them in context . . . [8]

A lack of primary source documents can vastly affect how a historical topic is portrayed. For example, one topic that I was supposed to cover in 5th grade according to my content standards was how state constitutions influenced the way our federal Constitution was written (California Content Standard, 5.6.5). Even though this is an entire subsection in the 5th-grade standards, not a single primary source state constitution is used in the textbook. We get a good idea why when we look at the actual texts of some of the state constitutions:

Massachusetts: Article II (1776). It is the right as well as the duty of all men in society, publicly, and at stated seasons to worship the Supreme Being, the great Creator and Preserver of the universe.

Delaware: Article 22 (1776) Every person who shall be chosen a member of either house, or appointed to any office or place of trust . . . shall . . . also make and subscribe the following declaration, to whit:

"I,_____, do profess faith in God the Father, and in Jesus Christ His only Son, and in the Holy Ghost, one God, blessed for evermore; and I do acknowledge the holy scriptures of the Old and New Testament to be given by divine inspiration."

Vermont: Frame of Government, Section 9 (1777) And each member [of the legislature], . . . shall make and subscribe the following declaration, viz.:

"I do believe in one God, the Creator and Governor of the universe, the rewarder of the good and punisher of the wicked. And I do acknowledge the scriptures of the Old and New

---

[8] *History–Social Science Framework for California Public Schools*, 2001 Edition with Content Standards, Appendix F, "Using Primary Sources in the Study of History"

Testament to be given by divine inspiration, and own and profess the protestant religion."

These are representative of a trend among state constitutions of that time, acknowledging God and, in particular, Christianity. It is important to note that these statements did not violate the (later) federal prohibition on a religious test for public office, that was included in the Constitution. Though *federal* representatives could not be required to pass a religious test, it was completely Constitutional for *states* to require their representatives to believe in certain Christian tenants of the faith. Publicly acknowledging God was clearly an integral and important part of every state constitution, and it is why our United States Declaration of Independence and Constitution acknowledge God so strongly.

One final example of a lack of primary source documents relates to the First Great Awakening. This is the name given to a series of religious revivals in the American Colonies during the mid-1700s. These "revivals" included an experiential presence of God, through a "filling" of the Holy Spirit, in those who attended. The First Great Awakening started in the middle colonies but quickly spread. It brought together many Christians across denominational lines and led to thousands committing their lives to Jesus Christ across all the colonies. There was some resistance within the established churches, but the vast majority of Christians felt that it was a mighty move of God among His body of believers. Preachers of the First Great Awakening included Jonathan Edwards, a Congregational pastor from Massachusetts, and George Whitefield, a traveling Methodist preacher from England.

A common thread that many historians observe about the Great Awakening is a passion for God. One of the most famous and instrumental sermons preached during the First Great Awakening was by Jonathan Edwards entitled, "Sinners in the Hands of an Angry God" (1741). As you can see, Mr. Edwards did not mince words:

> And let every one that is yet out of Christ, and hanging over the pit of hell, whether they be old men and women, or middle aged, or young people, or little children, now harken to the loud calls of God's word and providence.

According to several newspaper accounts at the time, people fell on their knees in repentance as Edwards delivered the sermon. After the services, cries could be heard from home to home throughout the town, from people who were calling out to God for forgiveness. People repented personally and corporately during the Great Awakening for forsaking God's providence and grace.

The historical records are clear: there was a mighty move of God throughout all the colonies in the mid-1700s, and this revival brought tens of thousands of Americans into a deeper, more committed relationship with the Lord Jesus Christ. The secular *World Book Encyclopedia*, 2004, says this:

> Great Awakening is the name given to a series of religious revivals in the American Colonies during the mid-1700's. Leaders of the Great Awakening included Jonathan Edwards, Gilbert Tennent, and George Whitefield.
>
> The Great Awakening had a strong influence on American religious life. It produced a new, excited form of preaching. The structure of worship services changed to permit increased participation by the laity. Elements of revivalism also became widely accepted as a means of converting people to a particular church. Revivalism emphasizes individual religious experience rather than the doctrines of a specific church.

The California Content Standard subsection 5.4.4, devoted to teaching about the First Great Awakening, says this: "Identify the significance and leaders of the First Great Awakening, which marked a shift in religious ideas, practices, and allegiances in the colonial period, the growth of religious toleration, and free exercise of religion."

Yet here's the only reference to the Great Awakening in my entire textbook:

> During the middle 1700s a religious movement known as the Great Awakening spread through the colonies. The Great Awakening, begun by Protestants, led to the founding of many other new colleges in the colonies.[9]

In one grand revisionist stroke, McGraw-Hill turns the First Great Awakening into a dull expansion of universities. They do

[9] *United States*, McGraw-Hill School Division, 1999, p. 247

not cite any primary source references in the textbooks. Their account starts off with some accuracy, but they quickly transform the awakening from a spiritual move of God, to an awakening of education. As stated previously, the colonists valued education deeply, but the Great Awakening was not an awakening of education, but of God in the hearts of the people. It was a spiritual revival, plain and simple. Also notice that the text only gives two sentences to an entire subsection of the content standards. As the federal court case was developing, my principal told me that I had no need to use any other supplemental materials in teaching history. She said, "You have everything you need in the district approved textbook. Use it." Most historians who have studied the Great Awakening would agree that the district-approved textbook was severely lacking in this area.

We can see from these types of historical revisionism that there is an "out of sight, out of mind" trend that is being played out in our culture. This trend is widespread not only in textbooks and public schools, but in the culture at large. Simply go to a museum, or watch the news, and you will see that there is an agenda to remove all references of our Christian heritage from public life. As we touched on previously, the phrases "One nation under God," "In God we trust," "Merry Christmas," prayer in Jesus' name, the Ten Commandments, and other religious expressions are all under attack by groups like the American Civil Liberties Union (ACLU), the Freedom From Religion Foundation, and Americans United for the Separation of Church and State.[10] This agenda is due to the improper reinterpretation of the Establishment Clause, and it has had a profound influence on our culture as well. By removing references to God from every arena of public life, it is easier for non-believers to ignore the whole subject of God, and for believers to fall into a more secular worldview.

God understands that we are visual beings. Think of all the references to memorials in Scripture, and the commands to "do this" to help us remember what the Lord has done. Organizations like the ACLU understand the power of the "out of sight, out of mind" principle. In Deuteronomy 6:6–9 we read this: "These

---

[10] Alan Sears and Craig Osten of the Alliance Defending Freedom, *The ACLU Vs. America: Exposing the Agenda to Redefine Moral Values*, Broadman & Holman, 2005

commandments that I give you today are to be upon your hearts. Impress them on your children . . . Write them on the doorframes of your houses and on your city gates." So the Israelites literally wrote the Ten Commandments on the doorframes of their houses and city gates. Yet by way of judicial activism that occurred in the 1980s (and not by the will of the people), the Ten Commandments were removed from all American public schools. Now they are starting to be removed from courthouses and public property, even though they are the foundation for our United States legal system. Remember what Joseph Story and many other Founders of our judicial system had to say about the foundation of our nation's morality? (See Chapter 2.) As these icons of our Judeo-Christian heritage are removed from public life, our nation's morality continues to decline, our history is revised, and people are becoming more secularized every day.

HISTORICAL REVISIONISM: HOW DOES IT HAPPEN?

Even though we have shown clear examples of revisionist history through biased presentation, omission, and lack of primary sources, there are many who still question whether our history is really being portrayed inaccurately. You cannot change what actually happened, right? So how does our history actually get changed and then institutionalized throughout the educational system and culture? Here is how it can happen.

If a scholar (someone who is considered an expert in a particular field) publishes a book that supposedly makes the case that we are more of a secular nation and that most of the Founding Fathers were Deists and not Bible-believing Christians, then that assertion can gain popularity, if not checked. Lies simply get passed on from one generation to the next through flawed "scholarly" conclusions. If someone is regarded as scholarly, than much of their work is simply accepted as accurate. Take W. E. Woodward, for example. He is a classic revisionist of the early twentieth century. His supposed "scholarly" work in the area of religious influence in American history has been parroted by numerous authors after him. In Woodward's book, *A New American History*, he falsely portrays the Founders, including George Washington, as being predominantly Deists rather than Christians, and as being greedily interested in making money.[11] He claims that George Washington might have mentioned God and had references to divine providence, but that Washington never mentions Jesus Christ.[12] Is that accurate? I hope you all are thinking, "No, that's not accurate." Remember what George Washington said to a group of Native American chiefs who wanted their children educated in American public schools: "You do well to wish to learn our arts and ways of life, and above all, the religion of Jesus Christ . . . Congress will do everything they can to assist you in this wise intention."[13] Either Woodward was ignorant of this fact, or he simply had an evil agenda. I will assume that it is the former, in which case it reveals a pathetic lack of quality research.

When you read the primary source writings of George Washington, it is clear that he was indeed a Bible-believing, sincere Christian. Professor Peter Lillback's book, *George Washington's Sacred Fire*, contains over one thousand pages refuting the false information that is perpetuated about Washington.[14] Even professors at secular universities applaud Lillback's efforts in their reviews. Walter A. McDougall, Pulitzer Prize-winning historian and professor at the University of Pennsylvania, said this: "[Secular historians] cannot ignore this mountain of evidence suggesting Washington's religion was not Deism, but just the sort of low-church Anglicanism one would expect in the eighteenth century Virginia gentleman." Robert P. George, professor at Princeton University, concludes that "Dr. Lillback buries the myth that Washington was an unbeliever—at most a Deist—under an avalanche of facts."

The real harm from revisionists like Woodward is felt decades later. Take for example, *The Religious History of America: The Heart of the American Story from Colonial Times to Today* by Gaustad & Schmidt.[15] I came across this book at my father's house. My father is a scholarly man who was a professor at Cornell

---

[11] W.E. Woodward, *A New American History*, 1937

[12] W.E. Woodward, *George Washington: The Image and the Man*, 1926

[13] George Washington, "Speech to the Delaware Indian Chiefs," 1779, published in *The Writings of George Washington*, 1932

[14] Peter Lillback, *George Washington's Sacred Fire*, Providence Forum Press, 2006

[15] Gaustad and Schmidt, *The Religious History of America*, HarperCollins, 2002

and likes to read academic materials on topics of interest. When I became a Christian and started Prepare the Way Ministries, he became more interested in finding out about an accurate account of our Christian heritage. Unfortunately, he likely based much of his opinions on books by authors like Gaustad and Schmidt, supposed experts in their field. Edwin Gaustad was a professor of history, and Leigh Schmidt received his Ph.D. from Princeton and was a professor of history at Harvard. I had never seen this book before, and my dad said that I should read it. I picked it up off the coffee table in his living room and started to read through it when I was visiting him one summer. The very first page that I providentially flipped to, about a quarter of the way into the book, reveled a disturbing trend that would later be confirmed. The history was inaccurate on many accounts and had a clear anti-Christian bent. On that first page that I happened to flip to, the author was discussing George Washington. I was immediately intrigued, having recently read many of his writings. You can probably guess what they said about George Washington: that he mentioned God, but never mentioned Jesus Christ! Gaustad and Schmidt were simply parroting what Woodward had claimed decades earlier, even though it was totally false. Their book is so widely used by universities and professors today that it is apparently required reading in most American religious history courses. So now we have students believing revisionist material and perpetuating it further.

In the example of *The Religious History of America* by Gaustad & Schmidt, the authors take a scholar's inaccurate account of our religious history (Woodward's) and assume it is accurate without (apparently) doing the research for themselves. Other scholars then take this work as accurate and add to it. Universities and schools use literature from these historically inaccurate sources in their courses and classes. And so the volume of historical revisionism increases. An entire generation of students are raised learning our history from these biased and inaccurate sources. Our history has been twisted to one that is more hostile towards Christianity. Yet one only needs to read the primary source documents themselves from our nation's history to see that this secularized history is false.

Another revisionist book by popular historians is *The Search for Christian America*, by Noll, Hatch, & Marsden. They claim to have discovered a severe lack of Christian influence in the founding of our nation. A very important question to ask is how they came to that conclusion. As it turns out, eighty percent of the "historical sources" which they rely upon to come to their startling conclusion were published in the late 1900s.[16] In other words, to "accurately" search for Christian America and what was happening in the 1700s, they primarily quote from modern works of the last few decades! Reading their book, one discovers a severe lack of primary source documents from the time period which they claim to be investigating. This is a selective use of primary sources, and a severe lack of sources from the very time period which they are researching. This is lousy scholarship.

Woodward, Noll, Hatch, & Marsden, Gaustad & Schmidt, and countless others, are pushing their agenda of revising American history. They use all the classic strategies employed by historical revisionists: a biased presentation of Christianity, omission of Christian reference from primary sources, and neglecting to use primary source references at all. Such books display a rampant eagerness to distort the Founders' original intention, that Judeo-Christian morals would shape our government. The actual writings of the Founding Fathers clearly show that they wanted Christianity to be strongly encouraged at all levels of American government and society. They did not desire to choose a particular Christian denomination, but they felt that Christian morality and a Biblical worldview needed to be the foundation on which our nation rested. They believed that without that foundation, we would surely fail as a nation.

History: Conclusions

Revisionist historians and textbook writers, who do not like the undeniable Christian heritage of our nation, are changing our history. This change is having a profound effect on our nation. Christians are becoming deceived by this changed history and sometimes even become ashamed of their faith. In addition, non-believers are becoming more hostile to Christianity because of this misrepresentation of our history.

---

[16] David Barton, *Original Intent*

When we as believers study the rich Christian heritage of the United States of America, we can be encouraged in our faith. Dr. Benjamin Harris proclaims in his book, *The Christian Life and Character of the Civil Institutions of the United States*, "[T]he American people should know the history and nature of the civil institutions of their Christian republic . . . and thus be qualified to discharge with fidelity and conscientiousness all the duties of an American citizen!"[17] To be a responsible citizen of this nation, we must study our history and be able to identify deception by historical revisionists. It is important to know the Christian roots of our nation when facing potential curriculum issues in public schools.[18] When Christianity is being portrayed in a negative light, we should step back and examine the author's agenda. Frequently, such authors leave out the positive contributions made in the name of Christianity throughout the history of the world.[19] History Professor Alvin Schmidt, Ph.D., has put together a comprehensive work in this area, titled *How Christianity Changed the World*. No accurate historian can deny that Christianity and Judeo-Christian principles have frequently been the source of massive amounts of goodness and progress in the world.

This is not surprising, since it was Jesus Christ who created the world and spoke all of creation into existence. It is He who holds the universe together today and is the source of every good and perfect gift. The reason there is evil in the world is not because of Christianity, but because of sin. Every bit of pain and suffering in the world is the result of mankind's prideful rebellion against God and His ways. As Christians, we can be confident in the truth that Jesus Christ has influenced the world more positively and more completely than any other person in history.

---

[17] Benjamin F. Morris, *The Christian Life and Character of the Civil Institutions of the United States*, 1864

[18] I would encourage everyone to utilize the excellent resources of David Barton and Wallbuilders in dealing with United States history. www.Wallbuilders.com

[19] Alvin Schmidt, *How Christianity Changed the World*, Zondervan, 2004

CHAPTER 8

CHART YOUR COURSE: PREPARE FOR CURRICULUM ISSUES—SCIENCE

I was in tenth grade. I started learning about evolution. It felt like my first window into the real world. To be honest, I think that learning about science was the straw that broke the camel's back. I knew from church that I couldn't believe in both science and God, so that was it. I didn't believe in God anymore. [1]

—Student Interview, *You Lost Me* by David Kinnaman

There is a common myth in our culture that science and Christianity are "at war." The false perception is that you must choose Christianity or science, but you cannot be in both camps. Many students gradually adopt this view due to textbooks, their peers, the media, or, sadly, through teachers who hold this worldview. For example, one public school textbook author said this, "By coupling undirected purposeless variation to the blind, uncaring process of natural selection, Darwin made theological or spiritual explanations of life processes superfluous." [2] In other words, this textbook teaches students, science has made Christianity and religion totally irrelevant. So if a Christian student is passionate about science, he or she may

---

[1] David Kinnaman, *You Lost Me: Why Young Christians Are Leaving Church . . . and Rethinking Faith*, Baker Books, 2011

[2] Douglas Futuyma, *Evolutionary Biology*, Sinauer Associates, 1986

feel the need to choose science over Christianity. This should never be the case, but sadly it happens all too often. The topic of science and Christianity has been explored in many excellent books, and there is so much information on this topic that we will only skim the surface in this book. The point of this chapter is to overview key topics that you can then study in more depth using other resources. Our goal is to make you aware of curriculum issues in the area of science that can most negatively influence your children's worldview.

ARE CHRISTIANITY AND SCIENCE REALLY IN CONFLICT?

A simple definition of *science,* based loosely on Webster's Dictionary, is "knowledge covering general truths or general laws, especially as obtained and tested through scientific methods." The scientific method is generally defined as a system for pursuing knowledge through formulating problems or asking questions, making hypotheses, collecting data that test these hypotheses, and drawing conclusions based on the data. Of course, these are simplified definitions and there are actually year-long college courses on the Philosophy of Science. For our purposes, we will go by the simple definitions. Now let's define Christianity. A simple traditional definition of Christianity is the religion derived from Jesus Christ, based on the Bible as sacred Scripture. So can someone who believes in Jesus also follow the scientific method by recognizing problems, making hypotheses, and collecting data? Yes, of course! Christians can plate bacteria, sequence DNA, and generally design and perform experiments as well as the next person. I (Sarah) spent many years wearing a white lab coat and working in a laboratory while getting my Ph.D. in environmental microbiology. In fact, many of the most famous scientists throughout history have been Bible-believing Christians, and they were pioneers in their various fields:

- Copernicus (1473–1543) Astronomy
- Sir Francis Bacon (1561–1627) Established the Scientific Method
- Johannes Kepler (1571–1630) Mathematics and Astronomy

- Galileo Galilei (1564–1642) Astronomy
- Rene Descartes (1596–1650) Mathematics and Philosophy
- Isaac Newton (1642–1727) Mathematics and Physics
- Robert Boyle (1791–1867) Chemistry
- Michael Faraday (1791–1867) Physics
- Gregor Mendel (1822–1884) Mathematics and Genetics
- William Thomson Kelvin (1824–1907) Physics
- Max Planck (1858–1947) Physics and Quantum Theory

All of these scientists were not only pioneers in their various fields of study, but were also committed Christians who firmly believed in divine creation.

The famous astronomer Galileo Galilei said "the Bible cannot err."[3] Isaac Newton reasoned that,

> The most beautiful system of the sun, planets, and comets, could only proceed from the counsel and dominion of an intelligent and powerful Being . . . This Being governs all things, not as the soul of the world, but as Lord over all; and on account of his dominion he is wont to be called Lord God.[4]

Since science is simply the investigation of the mechanisms of the physical and living world, there is no conflict between being a Christian and pursuing scientific knowledge. Christians can *do* science just as well as non-Christians; in fact, many of the most accomplished scientists throughout history, as well as in the present day, have been Christians.

WHAT IS THE TRUE SOURCE OF CONFLICT?

Since Christians can do science as well as non-Christians, why is there such a perception of conflict between science and Christianity in our culture? If you were to ask most people on the street if there is a conflict, they would likely say yes. The majority of conflict that arises between the Christian faith and science is not with science *per se*, though, but with the theory of Darwinian evolution.

---

[3] Galileo Galilei, "Letter to the Grand Duchess Christina of Tuscany," 1615
[4] Isaac Newton, *Mathematical Principles of Natural Philosophy*, 1687

The ironic part of this debate between Christians and evolutionists is that, in reality, evolution is a relatively small part of science. In fact, if you put evolution in its proper context, it is even a relatively small part of biology. Now to be fair, many biologists would say it is a large part of biology. However, as a professional biologist myself, I would challenge this assertion.

Evolution is a large part of the *past* narrative of how many scientists *believe* that life as we know it developed (although plenty of scientists disagree with the theory). The theory of evolution deals primarily with the *past*. Evolutionary theory is therefore unimportant and unneeded for the study of *present*-day, *practical* problems in biology, because most of the scientific work done in biology is with living creatures as they are today. So the practical work of a biologist (as opposed to theorizing about why something is the way it is) does not depend on believing in evolution, therefore biologists working in those fields don't need to believe in it. For example, in graduate school I studied how bacteria reduce the heavy metal Cr(VI) from its toxic state to its non-toxic state Cr(III). I studied certain bacteria that could perform these chemical reactions in the hope that scientists could harness this process in cleaning contaminated groundwater. However, even though my work dealt with molecular biology, I never once needed to reference or accept the theory of evolution. Doctors who cure diseases, biochemists who isolate enzymes, and microbiologists who study pathogens never need to use the theory of evolution in their experiments and research. Yet the false perception continues that one must believe in evolution in order to be a proper scientist.

Before we go on, it's important to make a distinction between macro-evolution and micro-evolution. *Micro-evolution* is a process that you can actually test in the laboratory or in field experiments. Micro-evolution describes changes in a particular *genus* or *species* of creature.[5] For example, over time a population of finches (to

---

[5] Matters of biological classification can get tricky, and scientists may have differing opinions on classifications. Normally an organism is named using binomial nomenclature, meaning its genus is named first, followed by its species (both in Latin so that scientists who speak different languages can all identify it). The name may be followed by a third subspecies name. To further complicate matters, the standards for genus classification are not strictly adhered to, so different authorities may produce different classifications for genera. Our point here is that although certain organisms

use a famous example) might develop slightly longer beaks, and biologists might then decide to call these long-beaked finches a separate species of finch. However, they are still the same type of bird; they are still finches. Also, these birds did not evolve into mice. They merely adapted, slightly, to their environment. (And if their environment changed back, their beaks would get shorter again—they would "un-change," or re-adapt.) Another example of micro-evolution would be bacteria developing antibiotic resistance. Imagine a population of some type (some *genus*) of bacteria that is suddenly exposed to an antibiotic. If one of these bacteria has a genetic mutation allowing it to survive that particular kind of antibiotic, this bacteria will be the "winner" in that environment. It will continue to live and reproduce while the others are killed by the antibiotic. The original population of bacteria will thus be replaced by an antibiotic-resistant strain. But they are still the same type of bacteria. The bacteria have not evolved into frogs.

In contrast, the theory of *macro-evolution* (which is what Darwin proposed and which is typically called simply "evolution") describes large jumps between very different kinds of creatures. Macro-evolution is a theory that attempts to explain the existence of all living creatures as we know them today, by starting with one simple bacteria-like organism. To state this more simply, *macro-evolution* asserts that life arose randomly, beginning as a single organism. It also explains that this single organism, through mutation and natural selection, evolved through a series of transitional species into all the species we see today. To use a simplified example: macro-evolution asserts that fish ultimately transformed into zebras.

Yet scientists have never actually observed one kind of creature turning into a completely different kind of creature. Scientists have observed micro-evolution, or adaptation, but never macro-evolution. No scientist has ever observed or scientifically documented Darwinian evolution.

---

might change slightly (through microevolution) under varying environmental circumstances, they still remain the same "type" of organism. The bird is still a bird. The bacterium is still a bacterium. However, scientists might then decide to classify it (i.e., name it), as a different genus. This name change does not mean that it has suddenly become a different "type" of organism.

What we will discuss in this section is macro-evolution. This is where the heart of the debate lies. No one is really debating micro-evolution, because we can see it in the laboratory. (For the sake of simplicity, from here on out we will simply refer to macro-evolution as *evolution.*)

So why is there a debate? The central issue is that evolutionists assert that life arose *randomly.* But the Bible clearly states that not only we humans, but all other creatures, were *intentionally designed with a purpose,* and made by God. So it is difficult for a Christian (and most other religious believers in the world) to believe in the entirety of evolutionary theory, because the word *random* is so intertwined with the definition.[6] Yet the God of the Bible is not random, but very intentional. This would not be a random process, but an intentional and design-based process, so there are some incompatibilities with traditional evolution.

The purpose of this chapter, however, is not to explore in detail the different camps with which Christians identify (broadly speaking, these are young earth creationists, old earth creationists, and theistic evolutionists). The purpose of this section is to point out where conflict may arise in public school, and to point you toward resources that can strengthen your faith. The purpose of this chapter is also to point out that if your family falls into the camp that questions evolutionary theory, your child should in no way be ashamed of that belief. As you will see, there are many large and legitimate holes in evolutionary theory—and scientific holes, at that—that make it completely reasonable to question it, even though evolution is taught as fact in schools today. We will discuss several of these holes, just so you are familiar with some of the key issues.

How Did Life Arise from Non-Life?

Most textbooks begin their narrative about evolution in a way similar to this, "All the many forms of life on Earth today are descended from a common ancestor, found in a population of primitive unicellular

---

[6] There are Christians who do believe in evolution; most would call themselves *theistic evolutionists,* meaning they believe that God guided the evolutionary process that created humans.

organisms . . . No traces of those events remain." One textbook says this, "Evolution—is not a theory. It is a fact, as fully as the fact of the earth's revolution about the sun. Like the heliocentric solar system, evolution began as a hypothesis, and achieved 'facthood' as the evidence in its favor became so strong that no knowledgeable and unbiased person could deny its reality."[7]

Public school textbooks present this information as if it were a proven fact, yet the origin of life is one of the strongest arguments that evolution is not at all a proven fact. Life is precisely one of the most compelling arguments for creation and *against* evolution. One of the most difficult aspects of trying to prove evolution is to prove how life arose from non-life. How exactly do you get a bacteria-like organism to simply "pop" into existence? Especially considering how vastly complex even the simplest life forms truly are?

According to the theory of biological evolution, life arose randomly around 4.7 billion years ago in a "primordial soup" that contained just the right chemicals in just the right environment to bring about the generation of a "simple" single-celled organism or bacterium. This bacterium was called the "progenote" or first living organism. According to the theory, the progenote evolved into other "transitional species" which through "random muta-tion and natural selection" would be better able to survive in their environment. Through billions of years and countless transitional species, life supposedly became more and more complex, eventu-ally resulting in humans.

However, there is no compelling evidence whatsoever for the progenote theory. The textbook I had to use while teaching a microbiology class said this: "What was the first self-replicating organism like? This question is impossible to answer at present."[8] To put it mildly, this is not your typical scientific language for describing something considered to be a "scientific fact"! Yet the scientific community frequently talks about evolution as if it were a proven fact and if you question it, people may look at you as if you were purple. Richard Lewontin, author and professor of evo-lutionary biology, says this:

---

[7] Douglas Futuyma,*Evolutionary Biology*, 1986
[8] M. Madigan et al., *Brock Biology of Microorganisms*, 10th Edition, Prentice Hall, 2003, p. 325

[E]volution is a fact, not theory . . . Birds arose from nonbirds
and humans from nonhumans. No person who pretends to have
any understanding of the natural world can deny these facts any
more than she or he can deny that the earth is round, rotates on
its axis, and revolves around the sun.[9]

Yet—notwithstanding Professor Lewontin's grandiose statement—proving how a progenote could have come into being is
impossible. Scientists can't do it, and saying they can doesn't make
it so. There is even vast uncertainty about the so-called "primordial soup." Michael Denton says, in his book *Evolution: A Theory
in Crisis*, "Considering the way the prebiotic soup is referred to in
so many discussions of the origin of life as an already established
reality, it comes as something of a shock to realize that there is
absolutely no positive evidence for its existence."[10]

Even assuming that we did know the right ingredients in
the "soup," it boggles the mind, even a scientific mind, to try to
comprehend how life could somehow magically materialize from
non-life. Even trying to imagine how to produce "merely" the
building block molecules required for life is mind-boggling. Sir
Fred Hoyle, Nobel Prize-winning British astronomer and mathe-
matician, set out to calculate the mathematical probability of the
spontaneous origin of life from a prebiotic soup environment.
Starting with the hypothetical primordial soup, Hoyle calculated
the probability of the spontaneous generation of *only* the proteins
of a *single* amoebae. Here is his conclusion: "The likelihood of the
formation of life from inanimate matter is one to a number with
40 thousand naughts [zeros] after it. It is enough to bury Darwin
and the whole theory of evolution."[11] And this is from an evolutionist! Professor Hoyle compared the odds of obtaining even a
single functioning protein by the chance combination of amino
acids to the odds of an entire solar system full of billions of blind
people . . . all managing to solve their millions of Rubik's Cubes
simultaneously.[12]

---

[9] Richard Lewontin, "Evolution/Creation Debate: A Time for Truth," BioScience,
volume 31 (1981), p. 559

[10] Michael Denton, *Evolution: A Theory in Crisis—New Developments in Science are
Challenging Orthodox Darwinism*, Adler & Adler, 2002

[11] Fred Hoyle, *Hoyle on Evolution*, Nature, Vol. 294, No. 5837, Nov. 1981, p. 148

[12] Fred Hoyle, *The Intelligent Universe*, Holt, Rinehart, and Winston., 1984

Even if we were able to create meaningful amounts of biological molecules (that is, basic chemicals required for life), it would be an entirely different matter to then somehow turn those bare molecules into a functioning, living organism. In another famous quote, Hoyle said that the probability of the spontaneous generation of a single bacterium "is about the same as the probability that a tornado sweeping through a junk yard could assemble a 747 from the contents therein."[13] And not only must there be some already existing mechanism to assemble the organism, but life by definition requires that that newly made organism must be complex enough to have the ability to reproduce, use energy, and respond to stimuli. Jonathan Wells, who has his Ph.D. from U.C. Berkeley in molecular and cellular biology, authored a book called *Icons of Evolution*. He says this:

> The problem of assembling the right parts in the right way at the right time and at the right place, while keeping out the wrong material, is simply insurmountable. Frankly, the idea that we are on the verge of explaining the origin of life naturalistically is just silly ... [14]

It is quite clear from these facts that—not only from a Christian perspective but also from an honest and objective secular perspective—the origin of life is indeed a miracle. And so far we have only been examining the formation of a single-celled organism, let alone an immensely more complex human being!

Based solely on the question of the origin of life (not to mention all the other huge scientific problems with evolution), it is clearly reasonable for any student to disbelieve that evolution is "proven scientific fact." Yet it is not uncommon for students to be labeled "ignorant" for doubting evolution in this regard. Many parents have told us of stories of their students feeling ashamed after teachers have singled them out or scoffed at their beliefs. In one case, the teacher actually had the nerve to call the student "ignorant." That is why it is very important for the dialogue between students and parents about curriculum topics such as evolution to be frequent and in depth. We have to warn our students that this type of persecution will likely arise so that it will not come as a shock.

---

[13] Ibid.

[14] Jonathan Wells, *Icons of Evolution: Science or Myth? Why much of what we teach about evolution is wrong*, Regnery Publishing, 2000

IRREDUCIBLE COMPLEXITY

Charles Darwin said, "If it could be demonstrated that any complex organ existed which could not possibly have been formed by numerous, successive, slight modifications, my theory would absolutely break down."[15] Michael Behe, author of *Darwin's Black Box*, challenged Darwinian evolution by theorizing that there are indeed complex organs that could not have been formed by "numerous, successive, slight modifications." He coined the term *Irreducible Complexity* in his book, saying this:

> By *irreducibly complex* I mean a single system composed of several well-matched, interacting parts that contribute to the basic function, wherein the removal of any one of the parts causes the system to effectively cease functioning. An irreducibly complex system cannot be produced directly . . . by slight, successive modifications of a precursor system, because any precursor to an irreducibly complex system that is missing a part is by definition nonfunctional.[16]

Examples of Behe's idea of irreducibly complex systems would be the bacterial flagella or the human eye; without each part in place, the organ would not have survived the evolutionary process because it would have malfunctioned, and so would have been a *dis*-advantage to the organism. Clearly it is fair for us in our day to question the reasonableness of an eye evolving. It is worth noting that secular scientists have popularized several counter-arguments to the theory of irreducible complexity. We need to be careful to think for ourselves. Simply because Wikipedia might make it sound as if the idea of irreducible complexity has been nearly disproven, I would not be quite so quick to bury the theory. Although this is a very complicated topic, it is a fascinating one. For those students who are science-oriented, it would be well worth their time to explore and make a personal evaluation of Behe's theory.

---

[15] Charles Darwin, *On the Origin of Species by Means of Natural Selection, or the Preservation of Favoured Races in the Struggle for Life*, 1859
[16] Michael Behe, *Darwin's Black Box: The Biochemical Challenge to Evolution*, Free Press, 2006

Transitional Species

The next major problem with the theory of evolution is this: *Where are all the transitional species it demands?* In Darwin's own words, we should be positively tripping over fossils of transitional species, and in every geological strata, yet this is not the case. Again, let's quote Darwin himself on this issue:

> . . . so must the number of intermediate varieties, which have formerly existed, be truly enormous. Why then is not every geological formation and every stratum full of such intermediate links? Geology assuredly does not reveal any such finely graduated organic chain; and this, perhaps, is the most obvious and serious objection which can be urged against my theory.[17]

In Darwin's time, geology was a relatively young science and geologists had only begun to unearth the fossil record. Yet even then, the actual science was all against Darwin's theory. What is interesting is that in the more that 150 years(!) since Darwin first made his claim, scientists have still not found anywhere near the "truly enormous" number of intermediate species that Darwin himself said his theory requires.

Some evolutionists have suggested that Darwin was wrong in his suggestion that there should be a gradual change from one species to the next through transitions. The theory called "punctuated equilibrium" says that species go through long periods of little or no change, and then suddenly go through radical, quick transformation, leaving little or no evidence of the change. The majority of evolutionists, though, reject punctuated equilibrium because there are so many difficulties with this theory. Ultimately, there are simply not enough transitional species to scientifically validate *any* evolutionary model.

Let's take a brief look at the topic of early humans. Undoubtedly, we have all seen the picture that has been around for decades, depicting a chimp-like species evolving into a modern man. But there are many serious scientific problems with this imagined human history, notably the so-named "missing links."

---

[17] Charles Darwin, *On the Origin of Species*

"The Ultimate Icon" illustration from Jonathan Wells's book, *Icons of Evolution*.[18]

A prominent authority on the "missing links," Erik Trinkaus, a paleoanthropologist from New Mexico University, writes about Neanderthal Man:

> Detailed comparisons of Neanderthal skeletal remains with those of modern humans have shown that there is nothing in Neanderthal anatomy that conclusively indicates locomotor, manipulative, intellectual, or linguistic abilities inferior to those of modern humans.[19]

In other words, as far as the experts can tell, Neanderthals were *not* "primitive" humans, but in fact were just as advanced and "modern" as humans today.

There have also been a number of questionable, and even fraudulent, "missing link" claims regarding how modern man evolved.[20] Here are some examples:

Java Man (1891). This was the first of many "proofs" for the evolution of mankind, which made huge news in the media. Eugene Dubois, in 1891, on the island of Java, Indonesia, found some remains somewhat close to each other and concluded that it

---

[18] Jonathan Wells, *Icons of Evolution*
[19] Erik Trinkaus, "Hard Times Among the Neanderthals," Natural History, vol. 87, December 1978, p. 10. See also: R. L. Holloway, *The Neanderthal Brain: What Was Primitive*, American Journal of Physical Anthropology Supplement, vol. 12, 1991, p. 94
[20] Jonathan Wells, *Icons of Evolution*

could be a missing link. It consisted merely of a skullcap, a femur, and three teeth. It is unknown whether those bones came from the same species, and even scientists of the time cast significant doubt upon the discovery's validity. Yet, Java Man is still written about in many science textbooks today.[21]

Piltdown Man (1912). Based on a "fossil" discovered in England, Piltdown Man was trumpeted as the missing link the scientists had all been looking for. Scientists discovered a human looking skull, with an ape-like jaw and teeth. It wasn't until 1953 that this skull was shown to be a fraud. A composite forgery, it consisted of a human skull of medieval age, the 500-year-old lower jaw of an orangutan, and chimpanzee fossil teeth. The forger stained the bones with an iron solution and chromic acid, and filed the teeth; these actions were what eventually caused him to be caught. Yet amazingly, Piltdown Man remains in some textbooks today as a "proof" of human evolution![22]

Nebraska Man (1917). Based on the discovery of a single ape-like tooth, evolutionists constructed an entire species, which they named "higher primates of the Western world." It was later realized that the tooth was a modern-day pig's tooth. The retraction in *Science* magazine ten years later, however, had only a fraction of the press coverage of the initial "discovery." Consequently, many textbooks today wrongly reference Nebraska Man as a "missing link."[23]

We can learn several key lessons from these "missing link" debacles.

First, some scientists were willing to *lie* about scientific discoveries. This is the highest abuse of science, as science is supposed to be about discovering the *truth* about how the world works. This dishonesty shows the religious fervor (irony intended) and deliberate bias of some evolutionists, including some today. Second, the cases of fraudulent "missing links" have *not* been widely publicized in textbooks or museums. This in itself is evidence of a significant bias: shocking stories like these should be widely broadcast in

---

[21] https://answersingenesis.org/human-evolution/hominids/who-was-java-man/. The AIG article also references Stephen Jay Gould's belief that the Java Man images found in textbooks today are "misleading."

[22] https://en.wikipedia.org/wiki/Piltdown_Man

[23] https://en.wikipedia.org/wiki/Nebraska_Man

the scientific world and memorialized as warnings. Students and everyone else should be made aware that these missing links were fraudulent and that the lack of genuine missing links weakens the case for evolution. Third, we need to be aware that some textbooks *still* refer to some of these fraudulent and dubious missing links *as if they were true*! We again refer you to Jonathan Wells's book, *Icons of Evolution*, for more information on this topic. You can also reference Wells's evaluations of unscientific bias in public school textbooks.[24]

Geologists who are evolutionists also have a serious problem. They cannot scientifically prove many evolutionary claims about the Earth's geological history. . . because there is simply no way to perform the required experiments. As a result, many evolutionary geology claims are nothing more than that: unfounded and unproven claims. As the textbook *Glenco Biology* (1994) instructs geologists: "To determine the age of the rocks, look to the kinds of fossils . . . to determine the age of the fossils, look to the kinds of rocks." This is nothing more than circular reasoning, of which there is a large amount in evolutionary geology. In addition, there is the problem that geologists are often drawing conclusions based on piecing together possible "clues" from the past, not actual proof from the present. It is important to keep all this in mind, and to warn students that there is a strong bias towards evolution and against anyone who might disagree with evolution.

INTELLIGENT DESIGN: AN ALTERNATIVE THEORY

The theory of Intelligent Design simply states that the vast complexity and order of all life is strong evidence for a designer. This designer is in contrast to the random process in the theory of evolution.

As scientists gain more and more knowledge, they continue to find that there is incredible structure and complexity within even the simplest forms of life. When we look at a space shuttle launch, we consider the complexity and intricacy of the design. We don't say, "Wow, how cool that it all just happened, by chance over time." In the same way, as scientists learn more about the

---

[24] http://www.arn.org/docs/wells/jw_tbookreport900.htm

amazing complexity of life systems, they see more and more evidence that there had to be a designer.[25]

As presented in public school settings by proponents of Intelligent Design, this theory does not even mention the subject of Biblical Creationism. It stops short of addressing the Biblical creation account and simply states that there is an increasingly large body of evidence for design in many fields of science. Yet this theory has caused abundant controversy. One school board asked for the following statement to be included in a science textbook:

> This textbook contains material on evolution. Evolution is a theory, not a fact, regarding the origin of living things. This material should be approached with an open mind, studied carefully, and critically considered.[26]

This reasonable statement was deemed a violation of the "separation of church and state" by the judges who heard the case.[27] In other words, these judges ruled that public school students should *not* think critically, nor study carefully, nor be open-minded to all the scientific evidence about evolutionary theory, whether for and against. These judges ruled that public school students must be spoon-fed an unproven theory that has many serious and recognized problems.

The consequence of this nonsensical ruling? Many young people feel ashamed in schools if they believe in a designer of the universe, and studies show that this intellectual shame is a leading cause of students walking away from their Christian faith. This is why parents and caring adults should take the time to help student think and study critically about this topic. An outstanding book in this regard is *Understanding Intelligent Design* by William Dembsky, Ph.D., and Sean McDowell, Ph.D.[28] We also encourage you to read Lee Strobel's *The Case for a Creator*. Strobel's book is a great place to start and provides a well-balanced, comprehensive study on this important topic.

---

[25] Stephen Meyer, *Signature in the Cell: DNA and the Evidence for Intelligent Design*, Harper Collins, 2009

[26] http://www.discovery.org/a/6401

[27] http://www.cato.org/publications/commentary/privatize-evolution-battle

[28] William Dembsky and Sean McDowell, *Understanding Intelligent Design: Everything You Need to Know in Plain Language*, Harvest House, 2008

HOSTILITY TOWARD INTELLIGENT DESIGN
AND THE CONCEPT OF CREATION

Many evolutionists are not content simply to debate the merits of evolution; they often feel the need to ridicule anyone who claims to believe in a Creator. Take Richard Dawkins for example, an atheist and leading spokesperson on evolutionary issues:

> It is absolutely safe to say that if you meet somebody who claims not to believe in evolution, that person is ignorant, stupid, or insane (or wicked, but I'd rather not consider that).[29]

One reason that there is a perception of such conflict between science and Christianity is due to scientists like Richard Dawkins, who seems to radiate hostility against God. Unfortunately, the many scientists who are Christians do not get the same kind of press.

The evolutionary movement has also taken on a religious fervor of its own. Nobel Prize-winning evolutionist George Wald was honest about his dilemma back in 1978 [emphasis added].

> There are only two possible explanations as to how life arose. Spontaneous generation arising to evolution or a supernatural creative act of God.... There is no other possibility. Spontaneous generation was scientifically disproved 120 years ago by Louis Pasteur and others, but that just leaves us with only one other possibility ... that life came as a supernatural act of creation by God, but I can't accept that philosophy because **I do not want to believe in God. Therefore I choose to believe in that which I know is scientifically impossible,** spontaneous generation leading to evolution.[30]

Another well-known American evolutionary biologist and geneticist, Professor Richard Lewontin, again echoes the tension he finds in examining the evidence:

> We take the side of science in spite of the patent absurdity of some of its constructs, in spite of its failure to fulfill many of its extravagant promises of health and life, in spite of the tolerance of the scientific community for unsubstantiated just-so stories,

---

[29] Richard Dawkins, "Put Your Money on Evolution," The New York Times Review of Books, p. 35
[30] George Wald, "The Origin of Life," *Scientific American*, Vol. 190, p. 46–50, 1978

because we have a prior commitment to materialism. It is not that the methods and institutions of science somehow compel us to accept a material explanation of the phenomenal world, but, on the contrary, that we are forced by our *a priori* adherence to material causes to create an apparatus of investigation and a set of concepts that produce material explanations, no matter how counter-intuitive, no matter how mystifying to the uninitiated. Moreover, that materialism is an absolute, for we cannot allow a Divine Foot in the door.[31]

The concept that there may be a designer is so unthinkable to many vocal atheists that they go on the offensive against Christians and anyone who dares to question evolution. Students must be prepared to face this type of opposition.

Why Should You Care?

Let's summarize why it is important to prepare your students for dogmatic opposition to the idea of a purposeful designer. First, the religious fervor concerning evolution has been used to attack the key Christian tenet that God is the designer of life. Second, many evolutionists' hostility to Christianity has damaged our culture's morality and our children's belief in God and the Bible. Third, the claims of evolutionists have greatly increased doubt among many Christians, especially our young people.

Many scientists, however, have found that their scientific studies have actually strengthened their faith in a designer. This can be the case for your student as well, if you take the time to dig into these issues. As Cambridge-trained author Stephen Meyer says,

> I look at the stars in the night sky or reflect on the structure and information-bearing properties of the DNA molecule, and these are occasions for me to worship the Creator who brought them into existence . . . I believe he has caused them to be unveiled in his providence and that he delights when we discover his fingerprints in the vastness of the universe . . . and in the complexity of the cell.[32]

---

[31] Richard Lewontin, "Billions and Billions of Demons," *The New York Review*, January 9, 1997, p. 31

[32] Stephen Meyer quoted by Lee Strobel, *The Case for a Creator*, Zondervan, 2004

Our hope is that the study of science will be a tool to strengthen your student's faith (since honest science does this), instead of being a stumbling block. But it will take caring Christian adults who are willing to invest their time to help guide students through the potentially tumultuous waters of today's public school science curricula.

CHAPTER 9

Chart Your Course: Prepare for Curriculum Issues— Literature/Sex Education/ Anti-Bullying/Holidays/ Common Core

Three philosophical threads weave through the Common Core—statism, moral relativism, and progressivism . . . Progressive educator John Dewey argued for standardized curriculum to prevent one student from becoming superior to others and envisioned a workforce filled with people of "politically and socially correct attitudes" who would respond to orders without question.[1]

—HSLDA and Henry Edmonson,
John Dewey and the Decline of American Education

Key Curriculum Issue: Literature

Literature is a difficult subject for parents to monitor. Who has time to read every book assigned to your child in class? This is where communication with your children can really pay off. It is worth the investment to ask your kids these three questions regarding their literature assignments: 1) Was there anything in

---

[1] http://www.hslda.org/commoncore/Analysis.aspx#FAQ. Henry T. Edmonson, III, *John Dewey and the Decline of American Education*, ISI Books, 2006

the story that made you feel uncomfortable? 2) Did you feel there was content that made you doubt your faith? 3) Would you have made decisions differently than any of the characters, and why? You will be surprised by the rich conversations that may develop. It is also helpful to do a quick search on some of the books that are assigned in class. Here are two great websites that review books: www.pluggedin.com (Christian), and www.commonsensemedia .org (not Christian, but a good site).

It is also wise not to miss an opportunity for a deeper discussion of books that lend themselves to faith discussions. For example, many 5th and 6th-grade classes read *The Lion, the Witch and the Wardrobe by* C.S. Lewis. Yet even though this book was written as a Christian allegory, many classroom discussions remain very superficial because of teachers' fears of violating the separation of church and state. When I was teaching, *The Lion, the Witch and the Wardrobe* was on the reading list and I always had an assignment where students could pick five of nine activities to complete. The year that I was under scrutiny due to the vocal atheist parent, I decided I would check with my principal about things that could be considered controversial. One of the questions that students could write about was how the novel fit the description of a Christian allegory. My principal was visibly annoyed and questioned why this topic was among the nine choices. I explained that I was using a well-respected supplemental reading guide that I had used for the past several years and no one had ever complained before. Although she did let me continue with the assignment, many teachers may avoid any potential controversy. This would be a great time to chat with your student's teacher and make sure that they are not avoiding topics in literature simply because they explore Christian ideas. It would also be useful with certain novels to get study guides from Christian school curriculum.

Because of widespread misunderstanding of the Establishment Clause, many school districts have increasingly purged books with Christian themes from reading lists and libraries. At a charter school in Southern California, a superintendent declared that the library would no longer be allowed to carry any "sectarian" (i.e., relating to religious sects) literature.[2] Pacific Justice Institute (PJI)

---

[2] http://www.wnd.com/2014/09/public-school-purges-christian-authors-from -library/#bpCC5g4ivvMFHEoS.99

President Brad Dacus says that among the books was *The Hiding Place*, the story of Corrie ten Boom, a Dutch woman sent to a Nazi prison camp during World War II for helping Jews escape. PJI wrote a letter to the public school that said a parent "was told by one of the library attendants that the library has been instructed to remove all books with a Christian message, authored by Christians, or published by a Christian publishing company."[3] PJI showed that the school violated the First Amendment and used an important Supreme Court ruling from 1982 to highlight this injustice:[4]

> Local school boards may not remove books from school library shelves simply because they dislike the ideas contained in those books and seek by their removal to "prescribe what shall be orthodox in politics, nationalism, religion, or other matters of opinion."

If you notice that certain books are being purged from libraries due to Christian references, initiate a discussion with your school's staff.

Even though literature is one of the more difficult subjects for parents to evaluate, it is worth the effort to stay involved. Kids are easily wrapped up in the emotional current of books as they identify with characters and situations. I (Sarah) remember as a child curling up in a rocker, tearing up as I finished *Where the Red Fern Grows*. Literature truly does open doors to new worlds, as the librarians always say. We want to make every effort to ensure that the doors our kids open are positive.

KEY CURRICULUM ISSUE: SEX EDUCATION/ ANTI-BULLYING

Another significant area that parents should monitor closely is sex education, anti-bullying, and other extra-curricular programs, all of which tend to have anti-Christian bias woven in. All schools have programs where they teach students about sexuality. In my district they called it *Human Growth and Development*.

---

[3] Ibid., see the Pacific Justice Institute's website for more cases that they are involved with, www.pacificjustice.org

[4] U.S. Supreme Court, *Board of Education v. Pico*, 1982

This is always done under the guise of simply teaching about the science of our physiology, but there are frequently moral judgments that are promoted during these lessons. This is not an area where parents should hand over the ship's wheel to the school. Teaching on issues such as sexual fantasy, masturbation, gender identity, sexual orientation, the definition of marriage, premarital sex, contraception, and others should be steered by parents. Yet all these topics are typically addressed in sex education materials presented in public schools. When a student's teacher and supplemental materials are presenting premarital sex as expected and contraception as a must, what is a student to conclude? Sexually Transmitted Diseases are presented in schools as just one of the risks we attempt to avoid using condoms (which frequently do not work against STDs such as HPV, human papilloma virus, and others).[5] Abstinence as a means for avoiding STDs and premarital pregnancy is increasingly minimized or even mocked. Sexual fantasies are presented as the norm, and the dangers of pornography are rarely taught. Of course most students will be swayed. Christians frequently feel ashamed of their worldview and are made to look like repressed "prudes." The truth is that God created sex for marriage and He is not a killjoy. Parents should present the topic of sex in a gradual and age-appropriate manner. Ultimately the final chapter of the story should be that God wants us to enjoy sex within the context of traditional marriage between one man and one woman (unless God calls you to be single).

Some people might argue that students are going to get challenged in their faith regarding sex at some point anyway, so why worry about it? I would argue that sexual topics are being presented at younger and younger ages in our public schools (to keep up with the general culture) to the point where children are not mature enough or wise enough to be able to logically defend their Biblical worldview. Usually as early as age 8 or 9 (it's getting younger every year), public school students will begin to be exposed to sex education. The curriculum includes supplemental videos, handouts, overheads, charts, and activities (most of which the students will not take home). The most controversial issues are

---

[5] The Institute for Research and Evaluation, *"Abstinence" or "Comprehensive" Sex Education?*, 2007

almost always brought up in the videos or in class activities. I think this is so that the districts will get the least amount of complaints; most parents simply do not have the time to watch all the videos, but could potentially scan all the written material. From a teaching standpoint, teachers (me included) love videos. With thirty-plus students in the class, what teacher would not want a brief break by periodically using a video? Other controversial topics may be presented in the form of a questionnaire, survey, or group discussion format, none of which generally get into the hands of parents. Take, for example, an actual 8th-grade classroom survey used in public schools:

> Adolescent sexual behavior instructions. Indicate in the space provided the minimum age at which each of the behaviors listed is considered appropriate or acceptable in your value system. In other words, when is it okay to engage in _____.
> [The behaviors listed include:] . . . kissing; French kissing; petting; masturbation; love making with a person of the same sex; getting drunk or stoned; seeing explicit sex in movies; having intercourse; having a variety of sexual partners; having an abortion; taking birth control pills . . . [6]

Notice the moral relativism in the wording of the question, "in your value system." After completing the worksheet, the students were told to get into groups and discuss their answers. These types of "surveys" are being used today; they clearly introduce deviant behavior in positive ways.

So how can parents proceed? First, it is critical to have the *dreaded* conversations about sexuality at home with your students. Parents should be their children's first sexual educators. Organizations such as Focus on the Family and Family Life have great programs and books to guide parents through the process.[7] Second, parents should consider having their kids opt out of

---

[6] Phyllis Schlafly, *Child Abuse in the Classroom*, Pere Marquette Press, 1993. Phyllis Schlafly, J.D., is Founder and President of Eagle Forum. Their Mission is to enable conservative and pro-family men and women to participate in the process of self-government and public policy making so that America will continue to be a land of individual liberty, respect for family integrity, public and private virtue, and private enterprise. www.eagleforum.org

[7] www.focusonthefamily.com; www.familylife.com

the sex education curricula. This is awkward, I know, but this is a legitimate option and parents have the right to pull their kids from the classes. Third, if parents opt to keep their students in sex education classes, ask to screen supplemental materials including videos. It is worth your time. Then follow up the classes with dialogue. Even if you pull your children out of the classroom, you need to realize that the sexual topics learned will now be at the forefront of every child's mind during this time. Therefore, there is a higher likelihood of recess conversations and interactions with other kids exposing your children to questionable ideas. Be prepared.

It is important to understand that not all sex education programs are bad. Most programs are based on what some would call "comprehensive" sex education, many of which are promoted and funded by Planned Parenthood.[8] The term "comprehensive" is generally a key word for including un-Biblical sexual behavior in the program. However, there are also quality abstinence-based sex education programs that are out there. Contrary to the "comprehensive" curricula, the abstinence programs are generally fairly solid, but not always. Again, do your research. In 2002, abstinence-based programs received $144.1 million in federal and state government funding, while "comprehensive" contraception-based sex-education programs received $1.73 billion.[9] For every $1 dollar spent on abstinence education, $12 was spent on "comprehensive" sex-education programs, such as those promoted by Planned Parenthood. Several studies published in peer-reviewed journals found that students participating in abstinence programs are more likely to delay sex or consider abstinence before marriage.[10] Research reported in the Journal of the American Medical Association by Dr. Michael Resnick *et al* in an article entitled

---

[8] http://www.heritage.org/research/reports/2004/03/facts-about-abstinence-education#_ftn14

[9] http://www.heritage.org/research/reports/2004/01/government-spends-12-on-safe-sex-and-contraceptives-for-every-1-spent-on-abstinence

[10] Weed *et al*, "An Abstinence Program's Impact on Cognitive Mediators and Sexual Initiation," American Journal of Health Behavior, 2007. Olsen *et al*, "The effect of abstinence sex education programs on virgin versus nonvirgin students," Journal of Research and Development in Education, 25:69–75, 1992. Jemmott *et al*, "Efficacy of a theory-based abstinence-only intervention over 24 months: a

"Protecting Adolescents From Harm: Findings from the National Longitudinal Study on Adolescent Health" shows that abstinence pledge programs are dramatically effective in reducing sexual activity among teenagers in grades 7 through 12. Based on a large national sample of adolescents, the study concludes that "adolescents who reported having taken a pledge to remain a virgin were at significantly lower risk of early age of sexual debut."[11] Parents should find out what kind of curriculum is being taught and should support solid abstinence-based programs. [12]

We also recommend finding out what kind of anti-bullying/"Safe Schools" programs or clubs exist at your student's school. First off, it is clear from the Bible that bullying is wrong. Teasing, verbally or physically abusing, belittling, and gossiping about *any* person is wrong and an awful witness for Christ. We are called in the Golden Rule to "treat others the way we want to be treated" (Matthew 7:12). Christians should be spokespeople and a shining beacon of light for treating others in a respectful way. Some anti-bullying programs are a non-issue and agree completely with a Christian worldview. However, there are increasing cases where either there is questionable material in anti-bullying programs or they are carried out in a misguided way. For example, Christians may be singled out if they actually speak about their belief in the traditional Biblical definition of marriage and sexual purity. One favorite label is "hater." Ironically, Christians can become the targets of bullying in the midst of anti-bullying programs. See Alliance Defending Freedom's valuable resource on this topic in Appendix E.[13]

We need to be aware that some anti-bullying programs are strongly influenced by people such as Kevin Jennings, former chief of the Office of Safe Schools in the U.S. Department of Education

---

randomized controlled trial with young adolescents." Journal of the American Medical Association: Pediatrics, 2010

[11] http://www.abstinenceassociation.org/faqs/

[12] The White House Office of Faith-Based and Neighborhood Partnerships, originally started by George Bush, is a way that Christian organizations can legally receive significant funds. See Alliance Defending Freedom's document titled "Government Programs FAQ" in Appendix E.

[13] Alliance Defending Freedom, "Anti-Bullying Policy Yardstick—A Guide to Good and Bad Policies"

under President Obama and founder of GLSEN (Gay, Lesbian, Straight, Education Network).[14] For one thing, Jennings has vocally supported and admired pioneering homosexual activist Harry Hay[15]. Harry Hay was an advocate of one of the most disturbing homosexual groups that is out there, the North American Man-Boy Love Association, or NAMBLA. According to the organization's website, Hay told the organization in a 1983 speech: "I also would like to say at this point that it seems to me that in the gay community the people who should be running interference for NAMBLA are the parents and friends of gays. Because if the parents and friends of gays are truly friends of gays, they would know from their gay kids that the relationship with an older man is precisely what thirteen-, fourteen-, and fifteen-year-old kids need more than anything else in the world. And they would be welcoming this, and welcoming the opportunity for young gay kids to have the kind of experience that they would need." NAMBLA advocates for the elimination of any "age of consent" restrictions and encourages sexual relationships between under age boys and men. Hay urged that NAMBLA be considered mainstream in America. In a transcript from a 1997 speech, Kevin Jennings said that he was "inspired" by Hay.[16]

What can we learn from these shocking statements? We can see that people of influence in the U.S. Department of Education may be on a drastically different moral page than you are. These are potentially some of the people who write, approve, and fund your student's school curricula. As a parent, you cannot have your head in the sand about what your children may be learning.

To summarize, we need to be aware of a growing trend that marginalizes parent's involvement in controversial subjects like sex education or other supplemental programs. We live in a culture where schools have frequently replaced parenting. We live in a culture in which adolescent girls can have a serious medical operation, such as an abortion, without their parents' knowledge or

---

[14] http://www.foxnews.com/politics/2009/12/14/obamas-safe-schools-czar-tied-lewd-readings.html

[15] http://www.wnd.com/2009/10/111792/#lv8CqzLUbBHrRK0t.99

[16] Americans for Truth chief Peter LaBarbera told WND the statements were transcribed from a tape of Jennings' address before a "Looking to the Future" panel at GLSEN's Mid-Atlantic conference Oct. 25, 1997, at Grace Church School in New York.

consent, but cannot even take an aspirin at school without parental consent (see www.protectourteendaughters.com). In many areas, schools have overstepped their bounds, and even good teachers and responsible administrators have limited power to counter the trend. Parents have the most power in this area and yet frequently do not realize it. Don't take this responsibility lightly.

KEY CURRICULUM ISSUE: HOLIDAYS

Holidays from all over the world are celebrated in public schools. Frequently teachers are applauded for teaching cultural diversity. Yet the applause suddenly ceases when the focus is on Christianity. Santa Claus, Easter bunnies, and other *faux* Christian symbols are generally tolerated. However, if you actually teach what Christian holidays are about, controversy may well arise. In contrast, other religious holidays are frequently described and presented in great spiritual detail.

When I taught 5th grade, we gave overviews of the major holidays from around the world: Ramadan, Diwali, Kwanzaa, Hanukkah, and Chinese New Year (which actually is a religious holiday), among others. When Easter came around, I thought it would be reasonable to do a lesson on this holiday, as I had covered so many others. When I presented the lesson to my principal, she became visibly annoyed and said that she would check with the district office. After checking with them she responded, "I was talking to the superintendent . . . and mentioned your assignment [on Easter]. He said, and I agree, no way. It does not relate to 5th-grade curriculum and standards." The timing of this conflict was interesting. The district had recently sent an email to all employees (over 1,200) encouraging them to attend a Hindu seminar. To provide an additional incentive, they offered to give professional development credit to anyone who attended. In effect, this is equivalent to paying teachers to attend, because teachers receive money for professional development credits. The website for the seminar described the material: "Embracing all creation like a divine mother giving love to her children. Accepting all, yet deferring only to the God of all creation . . . Hindu philosophy focuses on an all-encompassing reality of life as an interconnected

and current relationship with single force within all physical existence . . . We believe the Indian Culture and Hindu teachings offer
great promise to the world." The Cupertino Union School District
had no problem openly encouraging all staff to receive Hindu religious training, yet my simple, objective, 5th-grade class lesson on
Easter was barred.

Another local Cupertino middle school had organized a living
history month during Ramadan, in which the students learned
about Islam. The students pretended to be Muslims throughout the
day, which would include bringing their prayer carpets wherever
they went, praying five times per day towards Mecca, memorizing
the five pillars of Islam, learning about Mohamed's life and death,
and memorizing parts of the Koran and Hadith.

We see from these examples that many school districts may
endorse lessons and teacher training on other religions, yet there
is a double standard when it comes to Christianity. It was just
a short lesson about the National Day of Prayer, with several
primary source quotes from some key Founders, that escalated
the conflict in my 5th-grade classroom and eventually led to the
court case.

The National Day of Prayer is often ignored in public school
classrooms. Even though the President of the United States issues
a proclamation on the National Day of Prayer each and every year,
most teachers are afraid to discuss this holiday because of the supposed separation of church and state.

Yet prayer has been part of our government from the
beginning of our nation: this is why we have a National Day of
Prayer. From the records of America's first national Congress, in
Philadelphia on Sept. 5th, 1774: "Resolved, That the Rev'd. Mr.
Duché be desired to open the Congress tomorrow morning with
prayers." The next meeting the records are as follows: "Agreeable
to the resolve of yesterday, the meeting was opened with prayers by
the Revd. Mr. Duché. Voted, That the thanks of Congress be given
to Mr. Duché . . . for performing Divine service and for the excellent prayer which he composed and delivered on the occasion."

Reverend Duché's prayer was so moving, that many representatives of that early Congress wanted to make prayer a routine
occurrence at all legislative sessions. In fact, immediately after the
signing of the Declaration, they appointed Mr. Duché as the first

Chaplain of Congress and asked him to give the first prayer. Here is that first prayer, a prayer which started a history of opening every Congressional session in prayer:

> O Lord our heavenly Father, high and mighty King of kings and Lord of lords . . . over all the kingdoms, empires, and governments; look down in mercy, we beseech thee, on these American States who have fled to thee from the rod of the oppressor, and thrown themselves on thy gracious protection, desiring to be henceforth dependent only on thee; to thee they have appealed for the righteousness of their cause; to thee do they now look up for that countenance and support which thou alone canst give; take them, therefore, heavenly Father, under thy nurturing care; give them wisdom in council, and valor in the field; defeat the malicious designs of our cruel adversaries; convince them of the unrighteousness of their cause . . . All this we ask in the name and through the merits of Jesus Christ, Thy Son, and our Savior, Amen!

During a difficult time in the Constitutional Convention of 1787, Benjamin Franklin, addressing President Washington, stopped the proceedings and said,

> In the beginning of the contest with Great Britain, when we were sensible of danger, we had daily prayer in this room for the Divine protection. Our prayers, sir, were heard, and they were graciously answered . . . I have lived, Sir, a long time, and the longer I live, the more convincing proof I see of this truth that God Governs in the affairs of men. And if a sparrow cannot fall to the ground without his notice, is it probable that an empire can rise without his aid? We have been assured, sir, in the Sacred Writings, that "except the Lord build the House, they labor in vain that build it." I firmly believe this; and I also believe that without His concurring aid we shall succeed in this political building no better than the builders of Babel . . . I therefore beg leave to move that henceforth prayers imploring the assistance of Heaven, and its blessings on our deliberations, be held in this Assembly every morning before we proceed to business, and that one or more of the clergy of this city be requested to officiate in that service.[17]

---

[17] Benjamin Franklin quoted by John Eidsmoe, *Christianity and the Constitution: The Faith of our Founding Fathers*, Baker Book House, 1993

Benjamin Franklin is considered one of the least religious of the Founding Fathers, yet even he emphasized the importance of prayer in our nation's history.

Prayer was a regular occurrence not only in our nation's Capitol building, but throughout government and all of American society. In fact, the State became the Church in the early 1800s, in a manner of speaking. Actual church services were routinely held in the Capitol building during Thomas Jefferson's presidency; they continued to be held there until just after the Civil War. There were also many declarations of national days of prayer and thanksgiving throughout our nation's history. George Washington said this in a 1798 proclamation:

> Whereas it is the duty of all nations to acknowledge the providence of Almighty God, to obey His will, to be grateful for His benefits, and humbly to implore His protection and favour; and Whereas both Houses of Congress have, by their joint committee, requested me to recommend to the people of the United States a day of public thanksgiving and prayer, to be observed by acknowledging with grateful hearts the many and signal favors of Almighty God, especially by affording them an opportunity peaceably to establish a form of government for their safety and happiness.

Abraham Lincoln also issued a very famous 1863 Proclamation:

> Whereas, the Senate of the United States, devoutly recognizing the Supreme Authority and just Government of Almighty God, in all the affairs of men and of nations, has, by a resolution, requested the President to designate and set apart a day for National prayer and humiliation . . . and to recognize the sublime truth, announced in the Holy Scriptures and proven by all history, that those nations only are blessed whose God is the Lord.

My point in sharing these many quotes on prayer is that, despite this public promotion of a National Day of Prayer at the highest levels of our nation's government and by exalted national political leaders, most public schools will not let teachers even discuss this holiday, much less do lessons on it. Yet non-Christian holidays are highlighted, and many times the students are encouraged to practice them.

What can be done about this double standard? Parents and teachers alike have power to change this trend. By becoming educated about our Christian heritage, parents will know when these types of lessons are missing from the curriculum. The ministry, Gateways to Better Education, is spearheading a Holiday Restoration Campaign to encourage Christians "to help correct misinformation and restore accurate teaching of the religious nature of traditional American holidays."[18] Parents can sometimes visit classrooms and explain why holidays are meaningful to their family. Do not miss out on these opportunities to not only encourage your own students, but to encourage others as well. Make sure you are familiar with some of the documents in the appendices on students', parents' and teachers' rights in public schools.

Key Curriculum Issue: Common Core

The Common Core State Standards (often called simply "the Common Core") are two sets of K–12 academic standards that delineate what students should learn in English Language Arts and Mathematics each year, from kindergarten through high school. If states implement these standards, they receive increased federal funding. The Common Core has sparked widespread controversy throughout the nation. One reason behind the alarm is how quickly states hopped on board the Common Core ship. Rutgers professor Joseph Rosenstein commented, "Deciding so quickly, to me, is irresponsible . . . It was like it was a done deal, a foregone conclusion."[19] A second reason to take note is that educational standards, as we have seen in the preceding sections, have a large influence on the minds of our children. The Common Core centralizes educational standards, and therefore the federal government has more power over what kids learn. Many Christians desire less centralized government control, in which case states should have more say over their standards.

---

[18] https://www.gtbe.org/store/index.php/sku/4.html
[19] Catherine Gewertz, "State Adoptions of Common Standards Steam Ahead," *Education Week*, July 14, 2010

There is abundant information in circulation about the Common Core. The purpose of this section is not to provide an in-depth analysis of the problems with Common Core. Our aim is to make you aware of the larger issues so that you can keep watch for some of the negative influences of Common Core on your student's education. The Homeschool Legal Defense Association described the philosophical bias of the Common Core as follows:[20]

> Three philosophical threads weave through the Common Core—statism, moral relativism, and progressivism. The statist goals of the Common Core are implicit in the lockstep uniformity that is the central thesis of the program. Relativism's influence on the Common Core is evident in the open-ended and research-based assessment questions and the expansive new student tracking systems, ideas which have been strongly promoted by relativist Howard Gardner. Progressive educator John Dewey argued for standardized curriculum to prevent one student from becoming superior to others and envisioned a workforce filled with people of "politically and socially correct attitudes" who would respond to orders without question.[21]

Some parents and experts have been accused of overreacting to the Common Core. Yet within the context of this book, you can see what a profound effect the educational system has on the direction of our culture. We are talking about the minds of our children and the morals of the future generation. English philosopher John Stuart Mill wrote,[22] "A general state education is a mere contrivance for molding people to be exactly like one another . . . in proportion as it is efficient and successful, it establishes a despotism over the mind." We encourage you to stay up to date on Common Core issues. Voice your opposition politically, but until the standards are changed, be on the lookout for the three philosophical threads mentioned above.

---

[20] http://www.hslda.org/commoncore/Analysis.aspx#FAQ
[21] Henry T. Edmonson, III, *John Dewey and the Decline of American Education*, ISI Books, 2006
[22] Charles Leslie Glenn, Jr., *The Myth of the Common School*, ICS Press, 2002

Conclusions

We have seen throughout this book how public schools have been heavily influenced by a secular worldview. A Biblical worldview can be suppressed or discouraged in many different subject areas. We recommend investing in some Christian school or homeschool curricula to have available in your home as a reference through your journey.[23] To some degree, we are all teaching our children at home. It is difficult as a parent to stay in tune with everything that our students are learning. Yet being proactive about these subject areas is worth the time investment. As always, it is critical to find others to come alongside you in this endeavor. Keep dialogue open with other Christian parents in your school. If you find places of concern, share that information with others and take action that is rooted in love.

---

[23] www.preparetheway.us/Resources/links

CHAPTER 10

KEEP WATCH FOR
WORLDVIEW PIRATES

It's time to question the abuse of childhood innocence with
superstitious ideas of hellfire and damnation. And I want to
show how the scriptural roots of the Judeo-Christian moral edi-
fice are cruel and brutish . . . When it comes to children, I think
of religion as a dangerous virus.

—Atheist and author, Richard Dawkins, 1989

Nothing says *anti-Christian agenda* like a quote from Richard
Dawkins. When you read statements like the one above, it's
a reminder that there are those in the culture who would love
to "reform" your child's Christian worldview. While Dawkins's
quotes are some of the more abrasive out there in popular culture,
they do reflect anti-Christian sentiments that are commonly represented in public schools these days, especially in universities. It
is not a conspiracy theory that there are many groups so hostile
to the Christian worldview that they have organized efforts to
sabotage our young people's Christian beliefs. Unfortunately,
many of these efforts have been successful. As parents, it is wise
to take a step back and think about the "worldview pirates" that
our children might encounter and to help them navigate those
interactions wisely.

Teachers, coaches, friends, and many others make a significant imprint on your children. These key figures often have more

influence on this generation's worldview than we realize. A child can make a new friend and very quickly they may start talking and dressing like him or her. They may admire a certain teacher, and rapidly soak up their teacher's worldview. Clearly, children have different personalities. Some will be leaders and may not be as heavily influenced. Some kids will be more followers, and so might quickly mimic behavior and change their opinions.

The important warning for parents is to keep their eyes and ears open for the people who are important to their kids. The aim of this chapter is not to make us all paranoid. Our hope is to encourage you to fight for the heart of your child, or other children you care about. There is a delicate balance between protecting our kids and giving them freedom to grow. A parent's job is to wisely shepherd children away from wolves dressed in sheep's clothing (or openly dressed as wolves, for that matter). We all find that balance in different ways, and each family arrives at a different strategy regarding key issues. The purpose of this chapter is to make you think and pray about who is influencing your children, and to take action if necessary.

It is likely that you will have to take action on some level, either with a friend or teacher, or perhaps even the school district. We must remember that we are not fighting against people, but battling the worldviews by which they have been deceived. The following chapter has great detail regarding how we take action. The key points to remember as we encounter "worldview pirates" is that we must pray to be filled with love and the Holy Spirit so we can represent Christ well. Our ultimate aim is to represent Christ well in all circumstances.

Moral Relativism (Is North Actually North?)

Moral relativism and secular humanism often go hand in hand. Because secular humanism is now so prevalent in public school curricula, parents need to keep their eyes open for moral relativism surfacing in various subjects. We described this topic in more detail in previous chapters, but it is included here so that your "moral relativism radar" can be on, so to speak, as you are evaluating your children's school assignments.

Why is moral relativism so damaging to the faith of a young person? First, truth is knowable and immutable (unchanging). In contrast, moral relativists assert that we can never really know the truth. They say that truth is always changing, depending on the circumstances. But Jesus claimed to be *the* Truth. He said in John 18:37, "In fact, for this reason I was born, and for this I came into the world, to testify to the truth. Everyone on the side of truth listens to me." From a Christian worldview, it is clear that truth is knowable, and that Christ, and God's Word, are the sources of truth.

Second, we need to understand some basic rules of logic and reason. (Sadly, logical thinking is rarely taught in schools today.) There are unchanging laws of logic in regards to reason and thought. Entire courses are dedicated to this field of study, but for our purposes let's just look at one key law: the Law of Non-Contradiction.[1] This law simply states that a statement cannot be both true and false at the same time and in the same sense. In other words, if someone claims something is true, it cannot be both true and false, in the same context. For example, here is a clear truth claim that is foundational to the Christian faith and is an essential of the faith: "Jesus Christ is God incarnate." If someone denies this claim, they are not a Christian and we have a responsibility to share the truth with them. Here is another truth claim from Islam: "Jesus Christ is not God Incarnate." In fact, this is a big deal to all practicing Muslims; they consider it blasphemy to say otherwise. However, one statement is true and the other is false. The statements cannot *both* be true in the same sense. Whether it's Islam, Judaism, Hinduism, Buddhism, the New Age movement, atheism, or Christianity, all worldviews make exclusive truth claims about the nature of reality. They do not contradict one another on just a few points. They contradict one another on a majority of issues and almost always on key doctrinal points of their respective faiths.

Here are some truths about truth: truth is discovered, not invented. Gravity existed prior to Newton discovering it. Truth is universal and transcultural. Two plus two equals four for everyone, everywhere, at all time. It is always morally wrong to torture babies for fun. Truth is unchanging over time. When humans

---

[1] Kenneth Samples, *A World of Difference: Putting Christian Truth-Claims to the Worldview Test*, Baker Books, 2007

began to believe the earth was round, that new belief did not suddenly change the shape of the earth. All *truths* are absolute, but *beliefs* are relative. Beliefs can change, but truth does not. People can have contrary beliefs, but not contradicting truths. A final point is that truth is true, no matter how well or poorly it may be communicated.[2]

Next let's look at the issue of self-defeating claims. You've all heard them before: "there is no truth"; "all truths are half-truths"; "there are no absolutes"; "you can never know anything for certain." Christians must learn to lovingly and graciously show the clear error of these statements by pointing out that they are self-defeating. Apply each claim to itself and they fall apart. Each of these statements makes a universal or absolute truth claim, so it is actually claiming to be true. Someone says, "There is no truth." You should ask the person, "How do you *know* that statement is true?" Or, you could ask, "is that a *true* statement?" Here are common responses to each of these self-defeating claims:

All truths are half-truths. "Is that a half-truth?"

There are no absolutes. "Are you absolutely sure?"

You can never know anything for certain.
"Are you certain about that?"

My point is that these self-defeating statements are all foundational truth claims made by moral relativism. And since upon examination we can see that these claims are actually nonsense, therefore we see that moral relativism is based on nonsense. The Bible is clear in Psalm 119:160 (AMP): "The sum of Your Word is truth [the total of the full meaning of all Your individual precepts]; and every one of Your righteous decrees endures forever."

Moral relativism can be a hot-button issue in schools, but it needn't be. We just need to be able to—graciously—help people who have been deceived by the false claims of moral relativism to see the inconsistency of that worldview. One year while I was still teaching, the topic of morality came up during a planning meeting of upper-grade teachers. One teacher made the case that we should not address topics of morality because that was relative to one's

---

[2] Norman Geisler and Frank Turek, *I Don't Have Enough Faith to be an Atheist*, Crossway, 2004

faith and could potentially violate the "separation of church and state." That simple statement caused all the other teachers to agree. I was amazed. So now we could not even talk about lying, cheating, treating others the way we want to be treated, or any other moral claims? I decided I had to chime in. I asked which moral values we should avoid teaching on, and then listed the above. All the teachers then immediately saw the silliness of the one teacher's claim. It often just takes one person to speak the truth in love to make people take a step back and re-evaluate a situation.

TEACHERS WITH AN AGENDA

We want to say again that there are many wonderful teachers in our schools, both Christian and non-Christian. We should applaud the teachers in our lives for their tireless efforts and always be respectful of them, even in the face of opposition. That being said, there are teachers out there who do have an anti-Christian agenda, whether they know it or not. I certainly encountered them when I was teaching, and through our ministry I have counseled parents, staff, and students who have been negatively impacted by such teachers. Our recommendations on how to deal with such teachers are different for various levels of schooling.

In the elementary years, you should simply avoid teachers with an anti-Christian agenda, if at all possible. Students in these grades are typically with the same teacher the whole day. That teacher thus will have a huge influence on your child's worldview. If your child is assigned to a teacher who is known to be more hostile to a Christian worldview, we would recommend trying to switch classrooms if possible. You should request that your child be assigned to teachers who are positive towards Christianity. Most elementary schools will generally try to honor a parent's request for certain teachers.

In middle school and high school, on the other hand, switching teachers may simply be impossible. However, since students at these grade levels are usually in many different classrooms, one anti-Christian teacher may not have a significant influence. If you are faced with a teacher who appears hostile to the Christian faith, we recommend that you keep the lines of communication very open with your child about what they are experiencing in the classroom. If they feel uncomfortable or singled out for being Christian, then schedule a meeting with the teacher as soon as possible. There are more details on the appropriate steps outlined in the next chapter. One aspect of the situation that you should monitor is whether your student likes this teacher. It is almost always easier if your student is not fond of the hostile teacher. If there is a teacher that your student really admires, that teacher will potentially impress your student in many ways. Most of us can remember those special teachers who really inspired us. We want to make sure those special teachers are influencing your student in a positive way. If your child's favorite teacher starts teaching ideas that are contrary to your worldview, this is a tricky situation. You may have to handle those conversations with your child in a delicate way, as they may start siding with the teacher; your Christian worldview may suddenly become less popular than their hip favorite teacher.

It is generally fairly easy to spot the teachers with an agenda, and most Christians at a particular school will already know which teachers to avoid. For example, during my teaching career, I attended a training at a different school in another teacher's classroom. Though I never met this teacher, I knew that she was one to avoid. Instead of an American flag, she had posted a flag of "Mother Earth." Instead of the pledge of allegiance, there was the "Pledge to Mother Earth." Numerous other liberal icons were posted around the room. It was obvious that this teacher had an agenda, and was not afraid to push it.

Here is one last example about teachers with an agenda. A supporter of Prepare the Way Ministries called me one day with concerns about a high school teacher that her 16-year-old daughter had in a Western Civilization history class. The types of materials that the teacher had assigned showed an extremely anti-Christian bias; books by the likes of Howard Zenn[3] (a Leftist, Marxist professor and a prolific author) were the norm.[4] Yet this particular teacher not only had a very anti-American, anti-Chris-

---

[3] http://www.breitbart.com/big-hollywood/2010/02/04/howard-zinn-s-legacy-religious-fanaticism-and-illegal-indoctrination-of-your-children/
[4] http://spectator.org/articles/39155/case-against-howard-zinn

tian worldview—she was also one of the sweetest teachers in the whole school. The kids loved her! She joked around and had a bubbly, likable personality.

Although these situations can be the most difficult to deal with, this parent and family were solid Christians who were praying over the situation and who had a great relationship with their daughter. Their lines of communication were very open with her; if there had not been healthy communication, the mother would never have known there was an issue. However, the daughter felt comfortable enough with her mother to confide in her. They sought my advice in the appropriate steps for conflict resolution (we outline all these steps in the next chapter). The family exercised prayer and patience and spoke the truth in love. The matter was eventually taken up with the school board, and they agreed with the parent. The teacher was eventually reassigned. We can learn from this example about the importance of communicating with your child, and the influence that one parent can have.

COACHES

You might not think that coaches are a significant issue, but if you talk to kids and ask them about a particular coach, you may well find that your child has strong emotions about their coaches, one way or the other. Especially for kids who love sports, the coach-player relationship can be complex. If they develop a deep respect and attachment, a coach may have a surprisingly strong influence on your child. Long bus rides, numerous practices, and pep talks give coaches an opportunity to speak into the lives of young people. We see inspirational true stories of life transformation sparked by actual coaches in movies such as *McFarland USA* and *Woodlawn*. If your kids have positive coaches, perhaps even Christian ones, this may be a great blessing. A terrific ministry in this area is Fellowship of Christian Athletes.[5] You can check out their website to see if they are active at your local school.

However, if you get to know a coach and find they are fairly negative towards a Christian worldview, you should be on the

---

[5] www.fca.org

lookout for situations where kids are subtly or obviously teased or shamed. The relationship that students have with coaches can be tricky. If a child does not get along with a coach they may be benched; this can be very frustrating for both parents and students. The fear of this frequently causes students to avoid all possible conflict with their coaches. Find out what kind of advice or counsel your child's coaches are offering. If necessary, set up a meeting with a coach to discuss any issues of concern. Keep in mind the big picture: your child's spiritual and emotional well-being are more important than being on a particular team.

Friends and Peer Pressure

Many parents approach the teen years with apprehension, often knowing that a lot more peer pressure will suddenly hit. The Bible is not silent on peer pressure, though it doesn't use that name specifically. Proverbs 1:10,15 says, "My son, if sinners entice you, do not give in to them . . . do not set foot on their paths; for their feet rush into sin." Our culture is full of enticement, and the pressure escalates in the middle and high school years.

Friends can be a terrific or a terrible influence, and it may feel overwhelming to prepare for this season. I watched students in my classroom year after year soak up the influence of their friends like dry sponges soaking up water. An article in *Christianity Today*[6] makes a point that it is best to prepare early for peer pressure:

> Your child is on the brink of adolescence. Before long, he'll begin to separate from you. He'll appear less willing to communicate with you and more eager to turn to his peers for acceptance and ideas. Now, while your child is still receptive to your thoughts, take the opportunity to equip him to resist the onslaught of peer pressure so common to early teens.

We all know the storm is coming, but even before you see or hear it, there is much you can do. Most experts agree that many of the things we have already suggested in this book go a long way to

---

[6] "Preparing for Peer Pressure," Faith Tibbets McDonald, www.todayschristianwoman .com/articles/2001/november/preparingforpeerpressure.html

prepare for peer pressure: 1) prioritizing your relationships with your kids, 2) building a Biblical worldview early on, 3) preparing for peer pressure, and 4) cultivating positive Christian relationships with other role models, are among the top suggestions. Many parents tell us that it can also be very important to get to know your children's friends and their families. Make every effort to engage your kids' friends and get to know them. This not only allows you to be a positive influence in their lives, but also to find out if you sense any red flags.

If you are having difficulties with the influence of negative friendships in your kids' lives, you may want to refer to a book by Edward T. Welch called *When People Are Big and God Is Small: Overcoming Peer Pressure, Codependency, and the Fear of Man*.[7] Prolific author Dr. Kevin Leman also wrote a book with helpful advice on this called *Planet Middle School: Helping Your Child through the Peer Pressure, Awkward Moments & Emotional Drama*.[8]

We know from an adult perspective the truth and power of Romans 12:2, yet it can be extremely difficult for students in today's culture to obey it:

> Do not conform to the pattern of this world, but be transformed by the renewing of your mind. Then you will be able to test and approve what God's will is—his good, pleasing and perfect will.

We need to teach our children, in creative ways, that Christians are meant to be set apart, to think and act differently from non-Christians. We need to make sure our children know that we *do* understand how difficult this can be at times, but that they will experience great freedom and joy when they are not bound by peer pressure. Helping them find their identity in Christ is critical and the more solidly your child's identity is in Christ, the more likely they are to avoid risky behavior in general.

---

[7] Edward T. Welch, *When People Are Big and God Is Small: Overcoming Peer Pressure, Codependency, and the Fear of Man*, P & R Publishing, 1997

[8] Dr. Kevin Leman, *Planet Middle School: Helping Your Child through the Peer Pressure, Awkward Moments & Emotional Drama*, Revell, 2015

Media

The media in our culture today is like a hurricane. It can potentially shipwreck your child's faith, if you are not careful. The younger generation is massively connected to each other and the internet (phones, Facebook, Instagram, countless apps), and the media will capitalize on their connection in any way possible. More than one student leader who has been on our Christian Youth Summit leadership team has confessed to us that they "spent all night on Facebook." These kids were concerned that it was becoming an addiction. Woven throughout these apps and communications are marketing strategies that are trying to change your child's mind, in all kinds of areas. Movies, television, music, and magazines all send messages to our children's brains. How many of those messages are aligned with a Christian worldview? Not many. Being a parent myself, I sometimes literally feel like going Amish (but legalistically withdrawing from the world is not the Biblical way). The media hurricane is not blowing over any time soon, so we need to have our eyes and ears open.

The influence of the media on the younger generation increases with lightning speed each and every year. David Kupelian, author of *The Marketing of Evil*, notes how quickly the culture has changed:

> The plain truth is that within the space of our lifetime, much of what Americans once almost universally abhorred has been packaged, perfumed, gift-wrapped, and sold to us as though it had great value. By skillfully playing on our deeply felt national values of fairness, generosity, and tolerance, these marketers have persuaded us to embrace as enlightened and noble that which all previous generations since America's founding regarded as grossly self-destructive—in a word, evil.[9]

Those in the media often portray evangelicals as if they were a strange and curious alien species; something different from the norm; a separate breed. Kids acutely sense the pressure of being different. Although the Bible says that we *should* be set apart,

[9] David Kupelian, *The Marketing of Evil: How Radicals, Elitist, and Pseudo-Experts Sell Us Corruption Disguised as Freedom*, WND Books, 2005

this truth is often hard to live out. One *New York Times* article described the influence of the media on teens:

> Genuine alarm can be heard from Christian teenagers and youth pastors, who say they cannot compete against a pervasive culture of cynicism about religion, and the casual "hooking up" approach to sex so pervasive on MTV, on Web sites for teenagers and in hip-hop, rap and rock music. Divorced parents and dysfunctional families also lead some teenagers to avoid church entirely or to drift away . . . Over and over in interviews, evangelical teenagers said they felt like a tiny, beleaguered minority in their schools and neighborhoods. They said they often felt alone in their struggles to live by their Biblical values: avoiding casual sex, risqué music and videos, internet pornography, alcohol and drugs.[10]

TV shows and movies are frequently condescending towards Christians. Reverend David W. Key, director of Baptist Studies at the Candler School of Theology of Emory University, in Atlanta says, "Today, the culture trivializes religion and normalizes secularism and liberal sexual mores."

Author and speaker Mary Kassian attended one of Katy Perry's concerts and described her concern about the sugar-coated sexualization of young girls that is snowballing in our culture:[11]

> Perry joked about s-l-u-t-s and b**ches, sang about kissing girls, pretended to eat a pot-laced "brownie," and talked in code about getting drunk, partaking in sexual orgies, melting boys' popsicles, dissing parents, and having wrong things feel so right. She appeared in an endless parade of glittery, precociously sexual "little girl" outfits that focused attention on her breasts—with spinning peppermint candy plastered on them like targets, bras shaped like cupcakes and Hershey's Kisses, and even one that projected from the center of her nipples to shoot the audience with whip cream bazookas. The audience ate it up. The crowd, largely made up of screaming pre-adolescent and teen girls and their moms, matched Perry's candy-coated visuals of rainbows, hearts, and peppermint swirls.[12]

---

[10] http://www.nytimes.com/2006/10/06/us/06evangelical.html?ex=1317787200&en=51a7c2fe01e8148c&ei=5088&partner=rssnyt&emc=rss

[11] Mary Kassian, www.GirlsGoneWise.com

[12] www.crosswalk.com/family/parenting/katy-perry-and-the-sexualization-of-girls.html

I (Sarah) am stunned that more parents do not rise up and say, *Enough!* Instead, I continually meet Christian parents who "drink the Kool-Aid" and lock arms with the Katy Perry's of the world in an effort to fit in and please their kids. Here is a radical idea: listen to the lyrics of the songs that your kids are listening to. Talk about the lyrics. Look at their music collection. Draw boundaries. Be involved.

In talking to parents, we have observed that an effective way to counter some of these trends is to fill students up with positive media messages. There are outstanding, high-quality, Christian movies and shows out there. Find them and support their efforts. Focus on the Family has their radio show *Adventures in Odyssey,* with great stories that pre-teens enjoy. Listen with your children and talk about the episodes. There are terrific Christian books in every genre that have strong moral messages. Try to promote positive role models. Take your kids to Christian concerts. Go to places with a lot of other Christian kids so yours don't feel alone. Try to avoid the "drop off" culture and actually attend events *with* your children (for as long as they will let you). Buy your children music that backs up your worldview. Contrast Katy Perry's messages about sex and rebellion with Jamie Grace's lyrics below in her song *White Boots*:

> Little girl dreams are bigger than they seem . . .
> That's the kind of innocence that makes me wanna wait
> Until my wedding day
>
> Standing face to face with the love I know is true
> I'll promise him forever from the day we say, "I do"
> I've got my white boots
> My white dress
> And baby, I ain't getting them dusty

We live in a "dusty" culture. There is no easy formula to deal with the media hurricane. There is no magic submarine with which we can simply dive under it. We must not be in denial. The more proactive we are and the less "dust" we tolerate in our homes, the better off our children and our families will be.

The Internet

The World Wide Web has amazing resources that can strengthen believers and help us in our faith. It also has some of the most evil, pernicious, worldview pirates the world has ever known. There are real life pirates out there that want to capture your child's heart and destroy them. Schools are expecting children to navigate the internet at younger and younger ages. One key group of "pirates" on the internet deal in sexual immorality. Pornography is influencing young people in extremely negative ways. Studies have been on the rise showing the addictive nature of pornography, as well as the fact that younger exposure is more damaging. If you are thinking, *this is not an issue for our family*, consider these statistics and think again:[13]

- The **average** age for first time viewing of pornography is eleven years old.
- $97 Billion was spent on pornography in 2006, *larger than* the *combined revenues* of Microsoft, Google, Amazon, eBay, Yahoo!, Apple, Netflix and EarthLink.
- The largest group of viewers of Internet porn is children aged 12–17.
- 90% of 8–16 year olds have viewed pornography online (most while doing homework).
- Sexual solicitations of youth made in chat rooms and social media: 89%.

Needless to say, the pornography industry is huge, readily available to anyone, and it is easy for children to become accidentally entangled in it. The problem with internet pornography is the secrecy and lack of accountability. Before the internet, there were natural cultural barriers to pornography. For example, if a ten–year-old boy were walking in the red light district alone one evening, that would be a warning sign to many people, in and of itself. If that young boy decided to try to go into a porn shop and look through some of their material, obviously someone would confront the child. Now with the internet so accessible, children

---

[13] www.FamilySafeMedia.com

can view perversion without any accountability and in total secrecy.[14] Although not the subject of this book, I encourage Christians to take a stand on this issue and support legislation to protect our children.

Ted Bundy, an infamous serial killer, granted an interview to Dr. James Dobson of Focus on the Family, just before he was executed on January 24, 1989.[15] Bundy made some thought-provoking statements that we as Christians should take very seriously (emphasis added):

> As a young boy of 12 or 13, I encountered, outside the home, in the local grocery and drug stores, softcore pornography . . . From time to time, we would come across books of a harder nature—more graphic . . . Once you become addicted to it, and I look at this as a kind of addiction, you look for more potent, more explicit, more graphic kinds of material . . . Those of us who have been so influenced by violence in the media, particularly pornographic violence, are not some kind of inherent monsters. We are your sons and husbands. We grew up in regular families. *Pornography can reach in and snatch a kid out of any house today. It snatched me out of my home 20 or 30 years ago. As diligent as my parents were, and they were diligent in protecting their children, and as good a Christian home as we had, there is no protection against the kinds of influences that are loose in a society that tolerates pornography* . . . I've lived in prison for a long time now, and I've met a lot of men who were motivated to commit violence. Without exception, every one of them was deeply involved in pornography—deeply consumed by the addiction. The F.B.I.'s own study on serial homicide shows that the most common interest among serial killers is pornography.[16]

We see this in the media almost weekly: new cases of murderers or child abusers or sexual predators. The majority are heavily influenced by pornography. The most important message that Ted Bundy wanted to impart to our nation on his deathbed was that we, as a nation, should not tolerate pornography. We need to get the connection that Bundy was desperately trying to communicate between pornography and evil.

---

[14] Every home should be equipped with internet filtering. See www.covenanteyes.com
[15] www.FocusOnTheFamily.com
[16] Focus on the Family, "Fatal Addiction: Ted Bundy's Final Interview," 1989

CONCLUSIONS

Whether your child is a leader or a follower, it is crucial to be aware of who is important to them. Who are they paying attention to? Who are they admiring? Dr. James Dobson said this in a speech to the National Religious Broadcasters Convention:[17]

> Do you understand that children are the stem cells for the culture? The environment that you put them in is what they grow up to be. And if you can control what they hear, if you could control what they're told, if you have access to their minds . . . you can make them into just about whatever you want them to be.

It is wise to take our job of parenting and shepherding seriously. We need to be courageous in drawing boundaries in our homes between good and evil. Just as important, we need to teach our kids to draw healthy boundaries in schools and with their friends. That being said, we know of wonderful families who have tried to protect and teach their children, and they still had terrible difficulties. We are not passing judgment on anyone, but trying to exhort and encourage every parent to do the best job of navigation that they can. Continue to ask for and seek the Holy Spirit's help and guidance. Your children's hearts are worth fighting for.

---

[17] James Dobson, "Bringing up Boys," speech delivered at the National Religious Broadcasters Convention, Nashville, Tennessee, March 2002

CHAPTER 11

WHEN CONFLICT IS NECESSARY, SIGNAL FOR HELP

Instead, speaking the truth in love, we will grow to become in every respect the mature body of him who is the head, that is, Christ.

—Ephesians 4:15

While navigating the public school system, many potential conflicts can surface: with teachers, administrators, districts, coaches, or other students. Jesus warned that his true disciples would be persecuted for their faith. It is not a matter of *if* conflict will happen, but *when*. We are also commanded to be ready to give a logical argument for our faith. First Peter 3:15 (AMP) gives us guidance (emphasis added): "In your hearts set Christ apart as holy and acknowledge Him as Lord. *Always be ready* to give a *logical defense* for the hope that is within you, and *do it courteously and respectfully.*" Sadly, many Christians are unprepared to handle conflict in a Biblical way. Too often believers fall into one of two traps. They may avoid conflict at all costs. Or, they may try to engage in conflict unprepared and with the wrong spirit. It is tempting to become angry and agitated while engaging in conflict. That approach almost always ends poorly. God wants us to engage in conflict in a way that, if at all possible, helps lead others closer to Him. Our ultimate aim is not to win an argument or even to get certain school policies changed, for example. Our aim is to reflect the nature of God well and be good ambassadors of His Kingdom.

We learn from Scripture that we are indeed in a battle, but we must always remember that the battle is not against people ("flesh and blood"). In Second Corinthians 10:4–5, Paul reminds us, "The weapons we fight with are not the weapons of this world. On the contrary they have divine power to demolish strongholds. We demolish arguments and every pretension that sets itself up against the knowledge of God, and take every thought captive and make it obedient to Christ." The battle rages around us and we are constantly involved in it, whether we realize it or not. But this spiritual battle is never against people, but against false beliefs (any "argument" or "pretension" that is not in alignment with God's Word or a Biblical worldview). As we attempt to resolve any conflicts that arise, we must keep the gospel of Jesus Christ our central focus. With this in mind, in this chapter we summarize some key steps in conflict resolution.

SPEAK THE TRUTH IN LOVE

As always, our guide for our behavior and conduct is the Bible. A key Biblical principle on which to focus in the midst of conflict is to always speak the truth in love. Even though the truth might cause conflict, we must present the truth with grace, humility, and with our hearts rooted in *agape* love. Our overarching principles in resolving conflict are to reflect God well and to represent a winsome Biblical worldview. In all circumstances and with everyone, be calm and respectful. This is the way that we want to be treated, so we should aim to treat others in the same way. People are watching the way Christians behave, especially under pressure. I have seen too many Christians respond in inappropriate ways, which is a bad witness that can drive people away from the truth. The Bible says, "Be angry [but] do not sin." It is natural to become angry at times, especially in light of the increased persecution in our culture against a Christian worldview. This can be difficult to watch, and we can sometimes get righteously angry. But we must be careful not to let our righteous anger become unrighteous by expressing it in an un-Christlike way. Remember, we are not battling people, but the worldview that they have been deceived by.

During my court case, it was sometimes a challenge to speak the truth in love. One relationship was particularly challenging. News of the court case broke the weekend after Thanksgiving Day. Normally a quiet time in the media, this case somehow took on a life of its own. As the media frenzy surrounding my case was ramping up, I got an email from my principal saying that they were calling a special meeting for all staff, in response to the negative media attention that the Cupertino School District was receiving. At the meeting, my principal said that staff members should not be afraid to speak their mind about the negative media attention. As a result, I experienced a significant amount of hostility (although much support as well). After the meeting, I was talking with a supportive teacher when a hostile teacher came up to us. She was visibly angry and started to vent her anger at me: "How could you do this? You're a horrible teacher. You're a disgrace. How could you bring such negative publicity to our school?" By God's grace and strengthened by all the prayers being said for me, I was able to gently respond with phrases such as, "I hear you that you are angry. I would be happy to sit down and show you all the reasons why I felt it necessary to move forward with the court case." After more angry words, laced with profanity, this teacher summarized her feelings toward me: "I never want to talk with you, because you're a horrible person." She was so angry and hostile that, after she left, the other teacher said that I should file a grievance with the union over how she had treated me. Thanks to the Holy Spirit, I remained calm, and after the hostile teacher left, we prayed for her. This was the first of several tongue-lashings I received from this teacher in particular, as well as other teachers and parents. On one occasion, this same hostile teacher actually yelled derogatory statements at me across the school courtyard—with her students in tow, watching and listening.

Now to be honest, in conflict I am not normally the docile type. In fact, I would consider myself a recovering "type A" personality, and in the past I have struggled to respond lovingly to such mistreatment. However, God's grace, the Holy Spirit's guidance and much prayer allowed me to experience peace during this period of conflict, and remain calm and gracious.

Then one day, about three weeks into the court case, this teacher knocked on my door. When I saw that it was she . . . I sighed, expecting another berating. I prayed silently to God for help in handling her in a godly way. Fortunately, my students had just left. As I opened the door, I was surprised to see that she had a peaceful look on her face. When I asked what I could do for her, much to my astonishment she replied, "I've treated you horribly over the past several weeks, and I want to apologize about the way I've behaved."

I was in shock. This person, who had been so hateful to me, was actually apologizing—and of her own free will! When I told her that I totally forgave her and I appreciated her apology, she said that she was thoroughly amazed that I had never responded to her in an angry way. She asked me how I could stay so gracious and calm in the midst of all the pressure. An open door for the gospel? Absolutely. So I told her that my reaction was a result of my relationship with God, and that my wife and I had been praying for her. Later, this same teacher even told me that she had gone to church and that she was praying for me.

My point is that if I had—even once—gotten angry and responded to her in kind, I doubt she ever would have had a change of heart.

We must remember that we are ambassadors of Christ, and people are always watching us. On all occasions we must pray for the Holy Spirit to help us speak the truth in love, rooted in compassion and humility. We also need to be very careful how we talk *about* other people, even those who are persecuting us. A fundamental rule for Christians is that we must avoid gossip and slander. Even when people speak wrongly about us, we must never respond in kind. The Apostle Paul makes it clear that even though he was cursed by many people, he returned their curses with blessings. We are commanded to pray for those who persecute us, and even to love and do good to those who are our enemies. This is a daunting command from our Lord, but we must remember that we are filled with the Holy Spirit and thus we have all His power and love available to us. By His grace, we can always have total victory in how we treat other people.

Go Through the Appropriate Channels and Hierarchy of Authority

In addition to being ready for conflict and prepared to give a logical defense of the faith, we need to respect the appropriate channels of authority. If your child is forbidden by the teacher to read the Bible during free reading time, going to the school board to get the teacher fired or threatening a lawsuit should not be the first course of action. Nor should we threaten a lawsuit. Scripture guides us on how to handle conflict with passages such as Jesus's teaching in Matthew 18:15–17. Remember: every conflict happens for a reason and is an *opportunity* to share the gospel, the truth, and the grace of Christ.

Here are the appropriate steps for conflict resolution, in order. First, we go to the teacher, then the principal, then the school board and district offices. You will need legal advice along the way; don't delay in calling a Christian legal firm to get free sound guidance and resources.[18] (See the next section for more resources.) Many Christians mistakenly think that when they encounter any opposition, they must be outside of God's will. But remember, the Bible assures us that we will face conflict simply because we are Christians. We must learn that resolving conflict sometimes takes patience and persistence.

For example, suppose that a teacher does in fact tell your child that he or she is not allowed to read the Bible during their free reading time. Your child then comes home and tells you that the teacher said that reading the Bible at school is a violation of "the separation of church and state." Hopefully by now you realize that this teacher is mistaken because Christians, like all other American citizens, have a Constitutionally-protected right to live out their faith at school and to incorporate their worldview in every curricular area.

Our recommendation would be for your child to graciously submit to the teacher's request initially, but to politely let the teacher know that they will be talking about it with their parents. It is generally a good idea to submit to teachers, as long as they do not ask students to blaspheme God or compromise their Biblical

---

[18] Alliance Defending Freedom, www.adflegal.org

worldview or partake in something extreme. The student should then go home and talk it over with their parents and schedule a meeting with the teacher. The parents should bring with them materials that show the illegal nature of what happened (see the appendices for parents', students', and teachers' rights). If a satisfactory resolution does not come out of the meeting with the teacher, then the parent should request a meeting with the principal. If that does not yield a good result, then parents should contact the school board and district offices. Again, it is always wise to contact one of the Christian legal firms listed below to get free legal advice. Alliance Defending Freedom was the legal firm that represented me; they are an invaluable resource for believers in these types of situations. Many Christians do not realize that these firms offer their services free of charge. (We should prayerfully consider donating to these non-profits to help them continue their important ministry.)

It is also important that from the start you have a general idea of what your rights are (as a student, parent or volunteer, staff, or teacher). These rights are clarified in Chapter 6. Students have by far the most rights in public schools, followed by parents or volunteers, and then teachers and staff. We went into more detail in previous chapters, but the basic rule is this: **Students have the right to exercise their Constitutionally-protected freedom of religion and speech, at all times, in all curricular areas, throughout the entire school day,** as long as they do not materially or substantially disrupt the operations of the school or the classes.

Christians as well as the Christian worldview are being discriminated against in our public schools more and more. It is essential that you understand *that this discrimination is illegal.* Viewpoint discrimination breaks the law. In fact, if it can be shown that a public school is violating the federal guidelines[19] prohibiting viewpoint discrimination—they risk losing all their federal funding. Mat Staver of Liberty Counsel warns,

> School officials who choose to ignore the Department of Education guidelines risk losing their federal funding. Public

---

[19] U.S. Department of Education, "Religious Expression in Public Schools" and "Guidance on Constitutionally Protected Prayer in Public Elementary and Secondary Schools". See Appendix A and B.

schools must certify compliance with the guidelines annually with their state department of education. Each state must report non-complying schools. Complaints regarding schools not complying with the federal guidelines may be filed with both the state education office and the United States Department of Education.[20]

You must stand up against discrimination not only to protect your and your child's rights, but because you will be helping to protect the rights of *all* Christians involved in the public school system. Knowing and exercising your rights to freedom of religion makes a lasting impact on the entire system. This crucial struggle is not simply about your family; it's about advocating for those who come after you. If we Christians continually allow our freedom of religion and of speech to be taken from us, we could lose these precious rights altogether.

Following one of our seminars on "Navigating Public Schools" that we held in a local church, a pastor shared how someone in his congregation was empowered to live out their faith in school. The church was going to be hosting a Christian outreach at their facility. They had built a skateboard park on site and wanted to reach out to the young people in the area by having a BBQ and then sharing about Jesus. They made up a flyer and started to get the word out. One of the members of the youth group took the flyers to his 5th-grade class, since students were allowed to hand out birthday flyers and other notices that did not directly relate to official school business. The family was armed, in advance, with the important truth that whatever activities were allowed of a secular nature, the school had to allow similar activities, even when of a religious nature. So the family concluded, rightly, that their child must be allowed to hand out his church's skateboard event flyer.

Their son had given several flyers out during noninstructional time. When his teacher got a hold of one of the flyers, she immediately called him to her desk and with a stern look on her face, asked him about the flyer. The teacher wrongly told the student that the flyer violated the "separation of church and state" and then proceeded to confiscate all the flyers that had been

---

[20] Mathew Staver, *Eternal Vigilance*

handed out. She then sent the embarrassed student to the principal's office with the "offending" flyers in hand. After the principal backed up the teacher's false claim that this was illegal to do on school grounds, the boy agreed to stop handing the flyers out to his classmates.

When he arrived home that afternoon, the boy immediately talked with his parents. The parents then called their pastor for help. Empowered by the knowledge of their Constitutional and legal rights, they then asked for a meeting with the teacher and principal. At the meeting, the parents explained what the law actually says about their child's activities. Upon learning the facts, the school changed their decision. Not only was the boy allowed to hand out the flyer, but the school even sent it home to every student at the school in their weekly communication folder! Since the school regularly sent out other non-school related notices, they now saw that they also had to allow the church flyers. As a result of this family standing up and politely but firmly speaking out for their rights, many young people came to the church outreach, and some accepted Christ.

Becoming educated about your rights in public schools not only protects your child and their rights, but also empowers you to be a more effective evangelist and represent Christ better in your community.

SEEK FREE LEGAL HELP IF NEEDED

As we've mentioned, there are times when you should reach out to Christian legal firms. What an amazing blessing the Lord has given us, by providing these legal firms to represent Christians when needed! Alliance Defending Freedom was the firm that represented me during my court case; there are several others around the nation that are also there to assist Christians. The stated goal of each of these organizations is (to paraphrase their mission statements) to help Christians in all spheres of our culture to uphold a Biblical worldview and to influence the world around us with the gospel of Jesus Christ. I want to note again that most of their services are free. When I went through my court case, ADF represented me for free. This is their ministry. These groups exist due to donations and donors who believe in their work. If you ever have any questions about what you can or cannot do in the public school system as a Christian, please call them; they will give you wise counsel. They will help empower you to live out a Christian worldview and incorporate your faith in all areas of the public educational system and culture. Here is a list of some of these organizations:

- Alliance Defending Freedom, www.ADFlegal.org
- Liberty Counsel, www.lc.org
- Pacific Justice Institute, www.pacificjustice.org
- American Center for Law and Justice, www.aclj.org

BE UNIFIED IN THE BODY OF CHRIST

In order to have the most influence on our schools, we must work together in unity with other Christians. There is a huge benefit to students when they connect with other Christians on campus, regardless of their particular church or denomination. Parents will also benefit from connecting with other Christian parents. As long as someone is solid on the essentials of the faith, we can and should connect with them. These connections will strengthen students in their faith and help them make a greater impact at their school. It is crucial that we teach our children to have a heart of unity on the essentials and grace on the non-essentials. When our children attend school, they should be focused on being salt and light for the gospel of Jesus; they are not simply there to learn: they are also there to reflect Jesus Christ.

This message, of unity among believers, is woven beautifully throughout the Bible. Christians are meant to work together as a unified body, not as divided parts. The body of Christ includes all Holy Spirit-sealed Christians, both those within denominations and those who are non-denominational. Yet most Christians would admit that the body of Christ struggles to live this unity out.

Scripture is clear: it breaks God's heart that there is so much infighting and division among His children. The very first thing for which Paul rebuked the Corinthians church, was division: even before sexual immorality! Sexual sin, drunkenness, liberalism, legalism, and many other abuses were going on in the church in Corinth, but Paul dealt with their sins of division first, because division is such a powerful temptation and so terribly destructive. Immediately after Paul's introduction, he strongly corrects their sin of division (1 Corinthians 1:10):

> I appeal to you, brothers, in the name of our Lord Jesus Christ, that all of you agree with one another so that there may be no divisions among you and that you may be perfectly united in mind and thought.

Paul repeats his exhortation to unity three times in one verse! Whenever Scripture repeats itself, we should really listen up. In the original Greek and Hebrew, repetition was meant to emphasize a teaching. Paul goes on to explain exactly what he means, so there won't be any confusion: "My brothers, some from Chloe's household have informed me that there are quarrels among you. What I mean is this: One of you says, 'I follow Paul'; another, 'I follow Apollos'; another, 'I follow Cephas'; still another, 'I follow Christ.' Is Christ divided?" (1 Corinthians 1:11–13a).

Yet divisions like this are precisely what is happening within the Church today. One of you says, "I follow John MacArthur"; another, "I follow John Wesley"; another, "I follow John Calvin"; still another, "I only follow Christ, not organized religion." Is Christ divided? Certainly not! Paul then goes on for almost four chapters explaining why divisions are so deadly to our work and witness, and why we should be united on the essentials of the faith.

There may come a time when we should and must separate ourselves, but we must never separate from fellow Christians over the non-essentials of the faith. We should only divide on the essentials of the Christian faith or over unrepentant sin issues clearly stated in Scripture. There is always some debate on what the essentials actually are, but Christian theologians throughout history have almost universally agreed on them. Going back to the first century there have been clear statements of faith that Christians have agreed upon, such as the Nicene Creed, the Apostles Creed, and many others. If you look at almost any evangelical, Bible-believing

statement of faith today, they look virtually identical.[21] The essential truths of the faith will clearly answer these questions: 1) Who
is God? 2) Who is Man? 3) How do we know Truth? 4) Who is
Jesus? Any solid statement of faith should clearly define the answer
to these questions from a Biblical worldview.

If someone deviates on these core essentials, you have Biblical
grounds to lovingly divide over the issue. You should not remain
silent. But short of that, the Bible mandates that you be unified
with those who disagree with you on the nonessentials of the faith.
What are those? Some popular nonessential issues that frequently
cause division are the following: Arminianism versus Calvinism,
modes of baptism, gifts of the Spirit, the age of the earth, and end-
times eschatology. There are many others, but the key is to pray for
the Holy Spirit to guide us in unity and to have a loving, gracious
attitude toward everyone. Some visionaries of the Reformation
coined this phrase: Unity on the essentials, grace on the nonessentials, and covering over all . . . love.[22]

---

[21] This is Prepare the Way Ministries' statement of faith and it is virtually identical to
most any Bible-believing, evangelical organization. These are basically the "essentials
of the faith."

Statement of Faith
1. We believe that the Bible is the verbally inspired Word of God, without
error in the original writing, and the supreme and final authority in truth,
doctrine and practice.
2. We believe in one God, eternally existent in three Persons: Father, Son
and Holy Spirit.
3. We believe in the deity of our Lord Jesus Christ, in His virgin birth, in His
sinless life, in His miracles, in His vicarious death and atonement through
His shed blood, in His bodily resurrection, and in His personal return in
power and glory.
4. We believe that for the salvation of lost and sinful mankind, faith in the
Lord Jesus Christ and regeneration by the Holy Spirit are essential.
5. We believe in the present ministry of the Holy Spirit, by Whose indwell-
ing the Christian is enabled to live a godly life.
6. We believe in the forgiveness of sins, the resurrection of the body, and life
eternal and that Christians are called to be salt and light and fulfill the great
commission by reaching the world with the saving gospel of Jesus Christ.
7. We believe in, and seek to protect, the spiritual unity of the Church, which
is the Body of Christ, composed of all who are regenerated by the Holy Spirit
through faith, reliance, and obedience in the Lord Jesus Christ alone.

[22] http://www.equip.org/article/in-essentials-unity/

Bickering and gossiping within the body of Christ grieves God and is a poor witness to non-believers. Consider that Jesus prayed—*five* times—that we, the worldwide Church, would be one (John 17:20–23, AMP):

> I do not pray for these alone [it is not for their sake only that I make this request], but also for [all] those who [will ever] believe and trust in Me through their message, that they all may be one; just as You, Father, are in Me and I in You, that they also may be one in Us, so that the world may believe [without any doubt] that You sent Me. I have given to them the glory and honor which You have given Me, that they may be one, just as We are one; I in them and You in Me, that they may be perfected and completed into one, so that the world may know [without any doubt] that You sent Me, and [that You] have loved them, just as You have loved Me.

Why are we commanded by our Lord to be unified? "So that the world may believe." Jesus tells us that effective evangelism happens only when we, the entire body of Christ, are one. If we teach our children about the importance of unity in the body of Christ, they will be much more encouraged in their faith and much more effective at creating a community of believers within their school.

CONCLUSIONS

Most people dislike conflict. Yet Jesus warns us that when we follow Him, we are sure to face conflict in some fashion, at some point. But we need not fear conflict, knowing that God will "work all things for the good for those who love Him and are called according to His purposes" (Romans 8:28). God uses conflict to grow us and to make a difference in our spheres of influence. We are most effective when we work together with other believers, all throughout the body of Christ. Not only is this a better witness to the secular world, but it allows our gifts to complement each other as the Lord intended them to. Remember that the conflicts that often arise are not actually with people, but with worldviews (2 Corinthians 10:4–5). When we speak the truth in love and go through the appropriate channels of authority, we will have a far better chance of making a positive impact on our schools. Thankfully, if we do need to take a conflict to the next level of resolution, several excellent Christian legal firms offer free advice. When we engage in conflict, we must remember that our ultimate aim is not to win an argument, but to reflect the nature of God well and be good ambassadors of His Son and His Kingdom.

CHAPTER 12

RAISING OUR FLAG: INFLUENCING OUR SCHOOLS FOR CHRIST

You are the light of the world. A city on a hill cannot be hidden. Neither do people light a lamp and put it under a bowl. Instead they put it on its stand, and it gives light to everyone in the house. In the same way, let your light shine before men, that they may see your good deeds and praise your Father in heaven.

—Matthew 5:14–16

I conjure you, by all that is dear, by all that is honorable, by all that is sacred, not only that you pray but that you act.

—John Hancock

The purpose of this book is not only to exhort you to protect your child's worldview. Sarah and I also long for our Christian young people to *stand firm* in their faith so they can *stand for* truth in our culture. God's mission for all of us is to be His ambassadors, not simply to "stay Christian." It takes courage to forge ahead and take action. Sir Edmund Burke reminds us of an important stumbling block in taking ground: "All that is necessary for evil to triumph is for good men to do nothing." One of the most insidious stumbling blocks in our path is the temptation to simply do nothing. But the Bible does not depict God's people doing nothing. Jesus calls His followers to be empowered by His Spirit, and then to *do* something. The life of a follower is not a stationary life. The Bible calls us to be spiritually in motion: to pray, share the gospel, serve the poor, follow Jesus, heal, become equipped, and then equip others. Jesus does not want us to hide our light under a bowl.

START WITH THE INNER WORK OF CHRIST IN OUR OWN LIVES

To even begin to know where God is calling us to take action in our schools and culture, let's revisit the inner work of Christ in our lives that we touched on in Chapter 3, *Who is Your Family's Anchor?*

We will get overwhelmed if we mistakenly think that we are supposed to take action in every area where we see a need. We might also get stalled by indecisiveness: failure to narrow in on what we feel truly called to do can cause paralysis. We encourage you to pray about what assignment God is giving *you* in this season. Thankfully, we have the Holy Spirit as our counselor. We need only to pray and ask for the Spirit's guidance in our lives and He will give it. Luke 11: 9–13 (AMP) says:

> So I say to you, Ask and keep on asking and it shall be given you; seek and keep on seeking and you shall find; knock and keep on knocking and the door shall be opened to you. For everyone who asks and keeps on asking receives; and he who seeks and keeps on seeking finds; and to him who knocks and keeps on knocking, the door shall be opened. What father among you, if his son asks for a loaf of bread, will give him a stone; or if he asks for a fish, will instead of a fish give him a serpent? Or if he asks for an egg, will give him a scorpion? If you then, evil as you are, know how to give good gifts [gifts that are to their advantage] to your children, how much more will your heavenly Father give the Holy Spirit to those who ask and continue to ask Him!

We are assured that if we simply keep on asking Him, that we will be given good gifts, including the most important gift of all, the Holy Spirit. It is only by the Holy Spirit that we are born-again and are sealed for eternal life in heaven. It is only by the Holy Spirit that we can understand Scripture and be transformed to live a holy life for God. It is only by the Holy Spirit that we can influence our culture for Christ.

Our lives and ministries should look something like this: "Christ in us, doing an inner work" leads to "Christ working through us, doing an outer work." The outer work should always flow from the inner work that Jesus is doing in our lives. Trying to work from our own strength eventually leads to burn out, even if we are doing great things. Jesus cautioned His disciples before He ascended to Heaven, *Stay in Jerusalem until you are clothed with power from on high* (see Acts 1:8). What was that power? The Holy Spirit. In the book of Ephesians, the apostle Paul exhorts us to be "filled" with the Holy Spirit. The original tense of the verb "to fill" was in the Greek *continuous* tense. It was not to be a one-time filling, but a continuous process of being filled over and over. Jesus says He is the vine and commands us to abide in Him; the Holy Spirit is the sap in this spiritual vine. If we are not continually asking to be filled with the Spirit, acknowledging our dependence upon Him, our relationship with Jesus will eventually run dry.

I believe the church in America is struggling with issues similar to the church in Laodicea, as described by the Apostle John in Revelation 3:15–22:

> I know your deeds, that you are neither cold nor hot. I wish you were either one or the other! So, because you are lukewarm—neither hot nor cold—I am about to spit you out of my mouth. You say, "I am rich; I have acquired wealth and do not need a thing." But you do not realize that you are wretched, pitiful, poor, blind and naked. I counsel you to buy from me gold refined in the fire, so you can become rich; and white clothes to wear, so you can cover your shameful nakedness; and salve to put on your eyes, so you can see. Those whom I love I rebuke and discipline. So be earnest and repent. Here I am! I stand at the door and knock. If anyone hears my voice and opens the door, I will come in and eat with that person, and they with me. To the one who is victorious, I will give the right to sit with me on my throne, just as I was victorious and sat down with my Father on his throne. Whoever has ears, let them hear what the Spirit says to the churches.

The inner dysfunction of self-reliance led the Laodiceans to outer dysfunction in the form of selfishness and disobedience. We see the danger of wealth and pride in these verses. When we are poor and needy, whether financially, emotionally, relationally, spiritually, or in any other area, we are constantly aware that our next "meal" is coming from the hand of God, which makes us acutely aware of our dependence upon Him for our every need. The financially and technologically wealthy Western Church (and I can comfortably say that the majority of American churches fall into this category, relative to the rest of the world) too often fails to acknowledge its constant need for and reliance on Jesus. We then easily become more concerned about our own comfort than about serving God and other people. It is so tempting to idolize and trust in wealth and possessions and to forget our complete dependence on God. One of the vital first steps in intimacy with God is being acutely aware of our dependence on Him. Out of this realization flows a desire to be in the Word, to pray continually, to give thanks on all occasions, to become accountable, to practice forgiveness, and to follow Jesus passionately.

INNER WORK OF CHRIST SHOULD LEAD TO AN OUTER WORK

Having an intimate relationship with the Lord makes us more sensitive to the nagging feeling that something is missing when we are not "on a mission" for Him. Inner intimacy will inevitably lead to our being the hands and feet of Jesus in our culture. The problems with the church in Laodicea likely began in their hearts before it spread to the body as a whole. The passage indicates that they were more focused on pleasing themselves than on pleasing God. They were "off mission." Each of us has work and deeds that we are called to do, not to save ourselves, but because they are part of the mission the Lord has assigned to us personally. Ephesians 2:8–10 says: "For it is by grace you have been saved, through faith—and this not from yourselves, it is the gift of God— not by works, so that no one can boast. For we are God's workmanship, created in Christ Jesus to do good works, which God prepared in advance for us to do." We cannot forget that Jesus has given us a command: to do His works while we are on this planet.

So what are the works with which Jesus is concerned? We see from scripture that God cares about evangelism, making disciples, and caring for the poor and needy. Children in the public school system spend thousands of hours of their young lives there. We mustn't treat school like a separate sphere of their lives, where they leave their faith at home and just hope to fit in. School is a significant part of their lives, and your lives, as well. Therefore, it can be a place where they represent Jesus well and care about the things He cares about.

LINK ARMS WITH CAMPUS GROUPS

We spoke in an earlier chapter about what campus Christian groups can do for you and your kids. Research has shown these groups to be a powerful influence to help students on campus remain faithful to their Christian faith and make it their own. But here we want to focus not on what campus groups can do *for you*, but what your family's involvement can do *for Kingdom purposes*.

Many Christian researchers will tell you that the American Church has a consumer mentality. *What can the church do for me? What can church do for my family?* The Bible continually challenges us to flip that thinking on its head. God's Word teaches us that we are blessed when we ask, *What can my gifts do for the church?* Yes, the Church will meet many of our needs for community and learning, but God desires us to ask, *What can I do for God's Kingdom?* In our interactions with teens and young adults in public schools and college campuses, we have been alarmed that more students and parents are not asking this question. Many seem to view campus ministry only through the lens of what that group can do for them: *Do I like the kids involved, do I have fun, do I want to make time for it?* Those questions are not necessarily bad, but it is important to step back and look at the big picture and ask if God might be calling you to step out and be a part of what God is doing in your public schools. Many of these campus groups—Young Life, FCA, CEF, and others—are on the front lines on their campuses, so to speak. Their work is not easy, and their staff workers need the support of other Christians.[1]

---

[1] If your school doesn't have one of these groups, then please help start one. See Appendix C.

I (Sarah) was greatly helped by campus ministries during college and graduate school. I began seeking God in earnest during my junior year at the University of Michigan. My sorority roommate played volleyball, and she invited me to an Athletes in Action Bible study, even though I wasn't an athlete myself. She then started inviting me to her church. I felt that I was too busy, but I was intrigued and something strange was happening to me— God was tugging at my heart. I had so many questions. I attended a Veritas Forum[2] (a type of apologetics conference held on college campuses across the nation). One friend gave me the book *More Than a Carpenter* by Josh McDowell. I started reading it, and I was stunned to learn that there might actually be solid evidence for the Christian faith. You mean I didn't have to check my brain out at the front door of the church? This was news to me! By the end of college, I had one foot in church and one foot in the world. But when I traveled abroad to Oxford University on a fellowship, I thought I would put those questions of faith on the back burner. Once again though, Christian students and staff in campus ministry were actively involved on campus, and they wouldn't let me escape: I walked into one of the largest evangelistic outreaches in Oxford's history, organized by the Oxford Christian Union.[3] Again, many of my questions were answered. I finally became committed about my faith in Christ and came back to the U.S. a different person spiritually. I immediately moved to California to attend Stanford for graduate school. I looked for a campus ministry and became involved in InterVarsity Graduate Christian Fellowship.[4] I can honestly say that I don't know how I would have remained faithful to Jesus, or survived graduate school at all, without the support of InterVarsity.

God used various campus ministries to make a huge impact on my spiritual growth. There were several times when I was tempted to drift away from involvement. In high school and college, I had been used to (and idolized at times) being "popular." But the people with whom I hung out in the Christian circles on campus weren't always "cool" or my type, so sometimes I didn't

---

[2] http://veritas.org/
[3] http://oiccu.org/
[4] https://intervarsity.org/

want to be seen hanging around them. After a time, however, I recognized my attitude as snobbery, as pride. The Bible continually warns us against judging people based on their appearance or status, and I realized that I had fallen into that temptation. Thankfully, the Lord pointed this out to me, and I learned to be free from caring about being "cool."

So as someone who has struggled with this issue, I'm asking you to please gently point out to your children how often the Bible tells us not to judge people based on their appearance. We need to see the much greater vision, God's vision, of us being a Christian presence on campus.

BECOME AMBASSADORS FOR CHRIST

As we have mentioned several times throughout this book, we need to be mindful of *how* we take action. In conflict, we are commanded to "speak the truth in love" (Ephesians 4:15). Yes, speak, but do so in love. And what is love? It is worth reviewing again First Corinthians 13:1–8 for guidance:

> If I speak in the tongues of men or of angels, but do not have love, I am only a resounding gong or a clanging cymbal. If I have the gift of prophecy and can fathom all mysteries and all knowledge, and if I have a faith that can move mountains, but do not have love, I am nothing. If I give all I possess to the poor and give over my body to hardship that I may boast, but do not have love, I gain nothing. Love is patient, love is kind. It does not envy, it does not boast, it is not proud. It is not rude, it is not self-seeking, it is not easily angered, it keeps no record of wrongs. Love does not delight in evil but rejoices with the truth. It always protects, always trusts, always hopes, always perseveres. Love never fails.

Doing everything and saying everything in a spirit of love is critical for all believers. Otherwise we will sound like clanging gongs, Paul says. This does not mean that we will never offend someone. Even when we speak the truth in love, people can become offended. Jesus often offended people with the truth—but He never went out of his way to offend them. It was simply His truthful message that offended them. We may offend people with the gospel, but we should make every effort to communicate it in love. We should pray for wisdom in how we share God's plan of salvation within our spheres of influence, understanding that to some people it will sound like foolishness, but to others it will be a message that produces transformation.

We are called in Second Corinthians 5:18–21 (emphasis added) to be ambassadors, and with a ministry of reconciliation.

> All this is from God, who reconciled us to himself through Christ and gave us the ministry of reconciliation: that God was reconciling the world to himself in Christ, not counting people's sins against them. And he has committed to us the message of reconciliation. We are therefore *Christ's ambassadors*, as though God were making his appeal through us. We implore you on Christ's behalf: Be reconciled to God. God made him who had no sin to be sin for us, so that in him we might become the righteousness of God.

We are Christ's ambassadors. As we take whatever action the Lord calls us to take in our public schools, let us not lose the heart of Jesus's message—reconciliation—that is woven throughout Scripture. We must approach every situation with the wisdom of an ambassador and in a manner worthy of Christ. Have you ever heard of a silent ambassador? No! One of the main jobs of an ambassador is to talk to people in the country of their assignment. Our ultimate goal, though, is not to win an argument, but to win hearts. Greg Koukl of Stand to Reason summarizes the heart of ambassadorship in his excellent book *Tactics*:

> Finally, live out the virtues of a good ambassador. Represent Christ in a winsome and attractive way. You—God's own representative—are the key to making a difference for the kingdom. Show the world that Christianity is worth thinking about.[5]

Stand to Reason[6] provides many useful resources that will help you and your family become better ambassadors for Christ.

---

[5] Gregory Koukl, *Tactics: A Game Plan for Discussing Your Christian Convictions*, Zondervan, 2009

[6] www.STR.org

SILENCE EQUALS CONSENT

Dietrich Bonhoeffer, a Christian leader who took a stand against Adolf Hitler's totalitarian regime, said this:

> [Christians] are to remain in the world in order to engage the world in a frontal assault. Let them live out their vocation in this world in order that their unworldliness might become fully visible.[7]

Bonhoeffer wrote convictingly about the notion that *silence equals consent*. James 4:17 also warns us of this: "Anyone, then, who knows the good he ought to do and doesn't do it, sins." The Bible warns against Christians turning a blind eye to injustice. Christians frequently disagree on what qualifies as injustice, but we would do well to pray for wisdom about where and how to take action. We are all called to different assignments, but the body of Christ as a whole is called to move together on mission in our culture. Failing to act when you know of a violation of someone's rights in your community or an attempt to compromise someone's Christian worldview (no matter how subtly) is tantamount to consenting to it.

OVERCOME THE FEAR OF MAN

Many Christians (parents, students, teachers, all of us really) don't take action in schools or their culture because they are paralyzed by a fear of what others might think of them, say about them, or do to them. Our ability or inability to be salt and light in our schools and culture frequently comes down to how we answer this question: *Do we care more about what others think about us . . . or what God thinks about us?* Paul says in Galatians 1:10, "Am I now trying to win the approval of men, or of God? Or am I trying to please men? If I were still trying to please men, I would not be a servant of Christ."

The Bible exhorts us in numerous places not to be afraid, but in Proverbs 29:25 it is specific: "Fear of man will prove to be

---

[7] Dietrich Bonhoeffer, *Discipleship (The Cost of Discipleship)*, 1937

a snare, but whoever trusts in the LORD is kept safe." What is the antidote to the fear of man? Growing in our trust of the Lord. In Hebrews 13:6 (AMP), Scripture reassures us that we need not worry about what men can do or say: "The Lord is my Helper; I will not be seized with alarm [I will not *fear* or dread or be terrified]. What can *man* do to me?"

God has uniquely gifted you and placed you in this world to be His hands and feet and to represent Him well. All Christians are actually in full-time ministry. Whether you are paid or not does not make a difference; this is still God's purpose for you. The Bible makes it clear that we are Christ's ambassadors. Thus, all Christians have a Biblical responsibility to live out their faith in our culture and to represent Christ well. However, if we have a paralyzing fear of what other people will think of us, it will make us unproductive. The truth is that probably all of us, at one time or another, struggle with the fear of man. The important goal is to ask the Lord and other believers to help us overcome this fear. When students (and parents, teachers or staff for that matter) gather with other supportive Christians, they receive the critical support, courage, and boldness they need to walk in the calling God has placed on their lives.

One story from my court case illustrates how God can set us free from fear. About four weeks after the case began, smack in the middle of the media frenzy, a friend warned me to "be very careful with whom you are in your room alone." I asked him why I needed to be careful.

My friend told me that a group of parents were very angry about the negative reflection that the media coverage of the court case was having on the Cupertino School District. Some of these parents were saying that the case might negatively affect their property values. So they had organized a Yahoo online discussion group called "We The Parents." I discovered that there was one particular thread of messages from the group that went something like this: These angry parents implied that the ADF and I were telling lies about the Cupertino School District (which of course we were not doing). The goal of "We The Parents" seemed to be to show that the school district was a great one, while painting me as a Christian fanatic. Incredibly, some parents in this group said online that they were looking for someone who would be willing to say that I hit them or touched them inappropriately, or to make a claim that I did something illegal.

Discovering that these parents were putting out feelers to see if anyone would be willing to slander me and make a false accusation against me, fear gripped me to my core. Although some parents were very supportive of my stand, this particular group had turned out to be full of hate and intolerance. I had received hate mail, and my wife even received threats to our family. We had to call the police on one occasion, when we received what seemed to be a death threat. Given these shocking and totally unwarranted actions (almost unbelievable, actually), it was obvious that the hatred that some people felt toward me made a false criminal accusation a very real possibility. In my classroom I was alone with a student, parent, or staff person at some point every single day, and I knew that I was not smart enough to evaluate everyone's motive. So I had to face the frightening reality: proceeding with the court case could cause me to be falsely accused, put in jail, and possibly even to lose my family. Fear overwhelmed me. I went home and told my wife, and she was also overcome by fear. We wondered whether we should just drop the whole case. However, I knew that the Lord had called us to this fight and that He had given clear confirmations that this was the path we were supposed to take. That night, we both got on our knees and cried out to the Lord for what to do. And I mean I literally cried. I prayed fervently most of the evening and into the night.

The next morning I went to school still feeling very dejected and worried. My room mom showed up before any children had arrived for the day. She was a sweet Christian woman with four young boys at home. Ironically, she had vowed never to *be* a room mom, since she was so busy with her own children. However, in the beginning of that school year, she clearly felt the Lord call her to be my room mom. Praise God that she was obedient to that calling!

She came into my classroom that day and told me that the previous night, her mother had received from the Lord a long list of Scriptures to give me. During the very time that my wife and I were on our knees crying out to God and gripped by fear, her mother was writing down all the Scriptures that she felt the Lord wanted me to hear.

My room mom said to me, "I don't know all the details of what you're going through, but the Lord clearly gave my mother these verses for you." Then she handed me the list of Bible verses. My students hadn't arrived yet, and I felt compelled to read the list right away. I was amazed as I began to read:

> You are My servant—I have chosen you and not cast you off. Fear not, for I am with you; do not look around you in terror and be dismayed, for I am your God. I will strengthen and harden you to difficulties, yes, I will help you; yes, I will hold you up and retain you with My [victorious] right hand of right-ness and justice. Behold, all they who are enraged and inflamed against you shall be put to shame and confounded; they who strive against you shall be as nothing and shall perish. You shall seek those who contend with you but shall not find them; they who war against you shall be as nothing, as nothing at all. For I the Lord your God hold your right hand; I am the Lord, Who says to you, Fear not; I will help you!

These verses are all out of Isaiah chapter 41. And this woman's mother had written down three entire pages of Bible verses just like them!

As I was reading the verses, I felt the Lord's presence in a powerful way. I knew that it was God speaking to me through these Scriptures and through this grandmother, my room mom's mother. I started to weep, as I knew that the Lord was clearly telling me that I did not need to fear. God had my back. And if the Lord has your back, you have nothing to fear.

From that moment on, I knew that I never had to worry about the plans that the malicious parents were preparing. I knew at that time that "no weapon formed against me would prosper." It was miraculous how the Lord had given this woman parts of verses and different sections, yet all were written into one anointed word of encouragement that immediately broke off all fear from my life. After that moment, I simply did what the Lord had called me to do—and He protected me, my reputation, and my family.

My point is this: whatever the Lord calls you to do, whether it is something small like what I was called to do within the public school system, or something big, you do not need to fear. If you are in the Lord's will, He has your back. He will truly go before you and prepare the way for you. As we trust in the Lord more and more and with all of our lives, He will give us an amazing freedom to walk in the giftings that He has given us.

The Last Leg of My Court Case Journey

Throughout the court case, my aim was simply to request that the school district allow the use of primary source documents of our nation's history, even if they had Christian references. The response I consistently received from the principal and district was that they felt that the Christian references in those documents violated the alleged "separation of church and state." As time progressed, I think the school district was hoping that the case would simply disappear as soon as it was heard before the infamously liberal Ninth Circuit Federal Court. The date of the hearing was finally established for the spring of 2005, and we all showed up. The school district's lawyers were arguing for the case to be dismissed. My lawyers (from Alliance Defending Freedom) and I were arguing that we had a valid complaint.

The first major step in the case was for the judge to acknowledge that we even had a case to argue. Even I was a bit pessimistic that he would do this. As the judge was questioning the lawyers, my heart sank as his liberal bent was revealed. "We all know that the Constitution is a *living* document," he said, which is common language for a more liberal view of the Constitution. Yet even this liberally-minded, Ninth Circuit judge ruled that we did indeed have grounds to go forward with the case. He did not dismiss the case, as the school district had hoped. It was a tremendously satisfying moment in a tumultuous year.

Since the case had not been dismissed, I now had a choice. I could either go forward with the case and continue the legal battle, or I could now try to settle with the district out of court. After the motion to throw out the case was rejected, the district's lawyers were suddenly much more amenable to negotiating an out-of-court settlement. My wife and I prayed a lot about it, and we felt that the Lord was calling us to start a ministry. My wife and I were not seeking any financial gain, only a statement declaring that primary source documents were acceptable to include in public school classrooms, even if they had Christian references in them.

A settlement was agreed upon and filed in federal court that public school teachers could do just that. I felt great relief and satisfaction that other teachers and parents could now reference our legal settlement, whenever they faced similar issues in their schools.

As the case was being settled, I felt God's confirmation to leave teaching and go into fulltime ministry. It turned out that the "straw that almost broke the teacher's back" ended up leading this teacher down a different career path. I felt that the Lord wanted me to start a ministry to empower Christians when they are challenged in their faith. During the court case, I realized that when faced with a challenge that says, "This is a no-faith zone," many Christians were confused about how to take action. Whether the sphere is school, workplace, government, or the community, Christians need more support in upholding a Biblical worldview and sharing their faith confidently in appropriate ways. I started Prepare the Way Ministries in the summer of 2006 to encourage believers to uphold a Biblical worldview and influence an increasingly secular culture with the grace and truth of Jesus Christ.[8]

The Critical Component of Prayer

The challenges we Christians face in our culture are daunting. But as the Bible points out, when we are overwhelmed, we should always fix our eyes on Jesus. He is our strength and our source. When we cry out to Him, He will guide us to where He wants to use us for His purposes. As a body, we need to join together in humility.

Sarah and I are praying for a fourth Great Awakening in America. There have been massive moves of God and His Holy Spirit in the United States in previous times in this nation's history. During each of the previous Great Awakenings in America, millions of people came to Christ, denominational walls tumbled down, and the body of Christ worked together more in unity, covered in love. Each of these awakenings began when Christians had a burden to pray. We encourage the body of Christ will humbly pray together:

---

[8] www.PrepareTheWay.us

If My people, who are called by My Name, will humble themselves and pray and seek My face and turn from their wicked
ways, then will I hear from heaven and will forgive their sin and
will heal their land.

This passage, Second Chronicles 7:14, assures us that when
we join together in prayer for our schools and culture, God
promises to hear our prayers. Please pray with us for a massive
awakening of God's love and outpouring of His Spirit. We do
not deserve an awakening, but what a wonderful thing to see the
name of Jesus and His Word reverenced once more in our country.
Pray that the Lord would cleanse His bride of the sins of division,
unite us in reaching the world for Christ, and equip us to uphold
a Biblical worldview in our culture. We pray blessings on you and
your family as you navigate the public school system as "sailing
masters." May your family bring light and love and hope into the
darkest places.

RELIGIOUS EXPRESSION
IN PUBLIC SCHOOLS

The U.S. Secretary of Education sent a document titled Religious Expression in Public Schools to all public school superintendents to help clarify the appropriate inclusion of religion in our education system. We would encourage everyone to download this free pdf from our website.[1]

Here are some excerpts from that document:

"Student prayer and religious discussion: The Establishment Clause of the First Amendment does not prohibit purely private religious speech by students. Students therefore have the same right to engage in individual or group prayer and religious discussion during the school day as they do to engage in other comparable activity. For example, students may read their Bibles or other scriptures, say grace before meals, and pray before tests to the same extent they may engage in comparable nondisruptive activities."

"Teaching about religion: Public schools may not provide religious instruction, but they may teach about religion, including the Bible or other scripture: the history of religion, comparative religion, the Bible (or other scripture)-as-literature, and the role of religion in the history of the United States and other countries all are permissible public school subjects. Similarly, it is permissible to consider religious influences on art, music, literature, and social studies."

---

[1] www.preparetheway.us/Resources/downloads/

"Student assignments: Students may express their beliefs about religion in the form of homework, artwork, and other written and oral assignments free of discrimination based on the religious content of their submissions. Such home and classroom work should be judged by ordinary academic standards of substance and relevance, and against other legitimate pedagogical concerns identified by the school."

"Religious literature: Students have a right to distribute religious literature to their schoolmates on the same terms as they are permitted to distribute other literature that is unrelated to school curriculum or activities."

"Equal Access Act: Student religious groups at public secondary schools have the same right of access to school facilities as is enjoyed by other comparable student groups. Under the Equal Access Act, a school receiving Federal funds that allows one or more student noncurriculum-related clubs to meet on its premises during noninstructional time may not refuse access to student religious groups."

"Equal access to means of publicizing meetings: A school receiving Federal funds must allow student groups meeting under the Act to use the school media—including the public address system, the school newspaper, and the school bulletin board—to announce their meetings on the same terms as other noncurriculum-related student groups are allowed to use the school media."

As mentioned, to view the entire document, you may download it from our website.

APPENDIX B

GUIDANCE ON CONSTITUTIONALLY PROTECTED PRAYER AND RELIGIOUS EXPRESSION IN PUBLIC SCHOOLS

The U.S. Department of Education has also issued a document titled, Guidance on Constitutionally Protected Prayer in Public Elementary and Secondary Schools intended to further clarify the rights of religious expression in public schools.[1] Again, you may download a free pdf from our website, or see the link to the document on the Department of Education website.[2]

Here are some excerpts from that document:

"Among other things, students may read their Bibles or other scriptures, say grace before meals, and pray or study religious materials with fellow students during recess, the lunch hour, or other noninstructional time to the same extent that they may engage in nonreligious activities. While school authorities may impose rules of order and pedagogical restrictions on student activities, they may not discriminate against student prayer or religious speech in applying such rules and restrictions."

"Students may organize prayer groups, religious clubs, and "see you at the pole" gatherings before school to the same extent

---

[1] http://www2.ed.gov/policy/gen/guid/religionandschools/prayer_guidance.html
[2] http://www.preparetheway.us/Resources/downloads/

that students are permitted to organize other non-curricular student activities groups. Such groups must be given the same access to school facilities for assembling as is given to other non-curricular groups, without discrimination because of the religious content of their expression."

"Teachers, Administrators, and other School Employees: When acting in their official capacities as representatives of the state, teachers, school administrators, and other school employees are prohibited by the Establishment Clause from encouraging or discouraging prayer, and from actively participating in such activity with students. Teachers may, however, take part in religious activities where the overall context makes clear that they are not participating in their official capacities. Before school or during lunch, for example, teachers may meet with other teachers for prayer or Bible study to the same extent that they may engage in other conversation or nonreligious activities. Similarly, teachers may participate in their personal capacities in privately sponsored baccalaureate ceremonies."

"Religious Expression and Prayer in Class Assignments: Students may express their beliefs about religion in homework, artwork, and other written and oral assignments free from discrimination based on the religious content of their submissions. Such home and classroom work should be judged by ordinary academic standards of substance and relevance and against other legitimate pedagogical concerns identified by the school. Thus, if a teacher's assignment involves writing a poem, the work of a student who submits a poem in the form of a prayer (for example, a psalm) should be judged on the basis of academic standards (such as literary quality) and neither penalized nor rewarded on account of its religious content."

RIGHTS OF STUDENTS AND RELIGIOUS CLUBS IN PUBLIC SCHOOLS

Alliance Defending Freedom has put together a valuable resource that is concise and easy to understand, titled: Student Rights Handbook: A Guide to Constitutionally Protected Religious Freedom on Campus. Those involved in the public school system will benefit greatly from downloading this document.[1] The handbook is broken into four parts. Part 1: What Rights Do Individual K-12 Students Have to Express Their Faith at School? Part 2: What Rights Do Religious Clubs Have to Access Secondary School Facilities? Part 3: What Can Students, Coaches, and Teachers Do As Part of a Religious Club on Campus? Part 4: What Rights Do Students Have to Express Their Faith and Beliefs on College Campuses?

Below are some excerpts.

Student Rights

"Do students have the First Amendment right to express their religious beliefs at school?

Students retain their First Amendment liberties while on a school campus. They have the right to share their beliefs, pray, evangelize, read Scripture, and invite students to participate in such activities so long as they are voluntary, student initiated, and not disruptive or coercive. A school may not prohibit

---

[1] http://adflegal.org/issues/religious-freedom/k-12/resources

student expression during non-instructional time unless it (1) materially and substantially interferes with the operation of the school, or (2) infringes on the rights of other students. A school may not prohibit student expression solely because others might find it offensive."

"Can students express their religious beliefs during class or in an assignment?

While in class, students are free to express their religious views in a class discussion or as part of an assignment (such as an oral presentation or written essay), so long as the expression is relevant to the subject under consideration and meets the requirements of the assignment. School officials cannot prohibit religious expression in class unless they have a legitimate educational purpose for doing so."

"Can students distribute religious material at school?

Yes, students have the right to distribute religious and nonreligious material at school during non-instructional time. Of course, schools may bar any material that (1) materially and substantially interferes with the operation of the school, or (2) infringes on the rights of other students. But schools may not ban student literature distribution outright nor may they restrict literature based on its religious content or viewpoint."

"Can students advertise religious events at school?

Students may post signs on walls and bulletin boards and make announcements over public address systems about religious events at school to the same extent they may advertise similar secular activities."

"Do students have the right to engage in religious expression during school-organized events such as a talent show?

Yes, just as a student has the constitutional right to express his or her religious beliefs in a class assignment, he or she generally has the right to do so at a school talent show. This is especially true when the selection of the talent belongs entirely to the student and participation in the talent show is completely voluntary. Because the talent is the student's personal expression, and not that of the school, it is subject to full protection under the First Amendment. Therefore, students can sing and dance to religious songs and perform instrumental religious music."

In addition, there is an excellent FAQ (Frequently Asked Questions) page on ADF's website specifically helping parents and students.[2] It is a valuable resource.

Religious Clubs

"Can religious clubs hold meetings on campus?

In general, the [Equal Access] Act says that meetings of recognized non-curriculum related clubs, like religious clubs, may take place on campus 'during noninstructional time.' 'Noninstructional time' means 'time set aside by the school before actual classroom instruction begins or after actual classroom instruction ends.'"

"How may a religious club advertise for its meetings and other events?

Under the First Amendment and the Act, every club that meets the Act's requirements and is a recognized student club is allowed the same access to the school's facilities as every other recognized club. This includes access to public address systems, bulletin boards, the school newspaper, and other avenues that schools allow students to use to advertise meetings and other events. Students also have First Amendment free speech rights to distribute religious literature."

"Can religious clubs get funding from the school for their activities?

School funding for general student activities may come out of the Associated Student Body (ASB) budget or other student organizational funds that come from student fees. In that scenario, the school cannot discriminate against recognized religious student clubs by denying them equal access to funds simply because of their religious viewpoint."

"Can religious clubs have specific expectations of their members, such as they must identify as a Christian or must adhere to a certain code of conduct?

Yes, the First Amendment protects the right of student clubs to select their members and leaders based upon their adherence to the club's beliefs. The Supreme Court recently established that the First Amendment prevents the government from

---

[2] http://adflegal.org/issues/religious-freedom/k-12/faq

'interfering with the freedom of religious groups to select' those who 'convey [their] message and carry out [their] mission.' When religious student clubs select individuals who share their religious beliefs to be voting members and leaders, they are exercising this religious freedom. Thus, schools violate the rights of religious students by requiring them to abandon their right to associate with persons who share their beliefs as a condition to receiving recognition as a student club."

"Can schools place restrictions based on religious content?

Schools cannot censor the speech of student groups simply because the speech is religious. A school can only place restrictions on speech content if the regulation is necessary to serve a compelling state interest and the rules are narrowly drawn for that purpose. Schools cannot prohibit religious clubs from using religious words or symbols on their advertisements and other documents distributed to students, unless the speech causes a material and substantial disruption."

Students, Coaches and Teachers Activity in Religious Clubs

"What can a religious club talk about during its meetings?

Students are free to discuss any issues and engage in any religious speech they desire at meetings. The school does not have control over the content of the meeting, even though the meeting takes place on the school's campus. The school is obligated under the Equal Access Act and the First Amendment to provide equal access to all recognized student clubs, regardless of the content of their meetings, unless they 'materially and substantially' disrupt the educational process."

"Can religious clubs invite outside speakers to meetings?

Outside speakers are permissible at religious club meetings, and they can speak on any topic. A club inviting speakers to supplement their presentation must follow the school's policies related to recognized student clubs' use of school facilities."

"How much involvement can faculty sponsors have in religious club meetings?

Many schools require each recognized student club to have a faculty sponsor. It is fine for a teacher or coach to fulfill this role, but it must be done in a way that is 'nonparticipatory,' according to the Equal Access Act. This means that all of the activities that students participate in as part of the meeting are led by students, and the teacher or coach is only there to supervise."

"Is there a way a coach or teacher can actively lead and participate in a religious club?

Yes. A coach or teacher can lead a religious club if it is not a recognized school club. Whether or not a school district recognizes student clubs, it may allow its facilities to be used by community groups that have no affiliation with the district, such as the Boy Scouts, or various churches that may use school facilities during non-school hours. Religious clubs may request to use school facilities before or after hours as an independent community group. In that scenario, teachers may participate fully in meetings as individuals engaging in private speech, even if they are employed at that particular school. A school cannot restrict employees from participating in religious-based activities that occur on their own time, outside of school-sponsored events or instruction."

"Can coaches meet with other coaches and teachers as a group?

Even though school employees may not take an active role in meetings of recognized student clubs, teachers and coaches in public schools may exchange ideas or even have prayer meetings with one another, absent student involvement. If teachers are allowed to hold meetings unrelated to school business on the school premises, then they must also be allowed to discuss religion, pray with one another, etc., when there are no students involved."

THE FREE SPEECH AND ACADEMIC FREEDOM OF TEACHERS IN PUBLIC SCHOOLS

Alliance Defending Freedom has also put together this informative resource for teachers, administrators and all staff working in the public education system.[1] You may download it for free from their website below.

Here are some excerpts:

> "A teacher may objectively teach the Bible in a history of religions class or study the Bible as part of a literature course. The Bible can be taught in a school for its historical, cultural, or literary value, but not in a devotional or doctrinal manner. Sch. Dist. of Abington Twp. v. Schempp, 374 U.S. 203 (1963)."

> "When studying art, music, drama, or literature a teacher may objectively discuss, perform, critique, and overview religious music, composition, and history. 'Music without sacred music, architecture minus the cathedral, or painting without the Scriptural themes would be eccentric and incomplete, even from a secular view.' McCollum v. Bd. of Educ., 333 U.S. 203, 206 (1948) (Jackson, J. concurring). The Bible can objectively be used 'for its literary and historic qualities.' Schempp, 374 U.S. at 225. Teachers must simply mix the secular and the sacred. In other words, if a public school teacher presents a secular aspect

---

[1] http://adflegal.org/issues/religious-freedom/k-12/resources

along with the religious art, music, drama, or literature, then the presentation should be constitutional."

"Teaching about a religious holiday is permitted if it is part of a program of education which is presented objectively, and does not have the effect of advancing or inhibiting religion. For example, a teacher may explain that Easter is a religious holiday celebrated by Christians who believe that the person of Jesus Christ was raised from the dead. Historically, Easter celebrates the resurrection of Christ, whom Christians believe to be God. Done in an objective and educational manner, teachers can speak about religious holidays."

"Teachers also have some ability, though limited, to discuss alternatives to the theory of evolution, such as intelligent design. The Supreme Court has observed that 'teaching a variety of scientific theories about the origins of humankind to school-children might be validly done with the clear secular intent of enhancing the effectiveness of scientific instruction.' Edwards v. Aguillard, 482 U.S. 578, 594 (1987)."

"[I]f teachers are permitted to post or distribute flyers for non-curricular activities or announcements in the faculty lounge or in teachers' school mailboxes, then religious events and activities may be publicized to other staff members in the same manner."

"Some schools allow teachers to utilize a classroom or a lounge to meet with other teachers. If the school allows teachers to use school facilities for secular meetings, then the school must also allow teachers to use school facilities for religious meetings. The school may restrict the use of its facilities by teachers for only class-related meetings or topics. If the school allows teach-ers to use its facilities for non-curriculum related matters such as socialization and entertainment, then teachers should also be able to use the same facilities for Bible study and prayer. In this case only teachers should be in the meeting, not students."

"Nearly every public school enforces policies that regu-late teacher conduct and speech. Sometimes these policies use vague and overbroad words that give administrators virtually unlimited discretion. A government policy is unconstitutionally vague when it (1) denies professors fair notice of the stan-dard of expression to which they are accountable; (2) permits unrestricted enforcement against any professor at anytime, thereby inviting arbitrary, discriminatory and overzealous enforcement; and (3) chills the exercise of First Amendment freedoms."

In addition, there is an excellent FAQ (Frequently Asked Questions) page on ADF's website specifically helping teachers.[2]

---

[2] http://adflegal.org/issues/religious-freedom/k-12/faq

APPENDIX E

FURTHER RESOURCES ON RIGHTS IN THE PUBLIC SCHOOL SYSTEM

Alliance Defending Freedom has a variety of other resource on other subjects that are free to download on their website.[1]
Here is a list of some of the titles:

- Constitutionality of Prayer at High School Graduation/Baccalaureate
- Government Programs FAQ
- Anti-Bullying Policy Yardstick—A Guide to Good and Bad Policies
- Freedom of Association—Public Schools
- Equal Access—Public Schools
- Freedom of Speech—Public Schools
- Freedom to Exercise Religious Beliefs—Public Schools

---

[1] http://adflegal.org/issues/religious-freedom/k-12/resources

DECLARATION OF INDEPENDENCE

IN CONGRESS, July 4, 1776.

The unanimous Declaration of the thirteen united States of America,

When in the Course of human events, it becomes necessary for one people to dissolve the political bands which have connected them with another, and to assume among the powers of the earth, the separate and equal station to which the Laws of Nature and of Nature's God entitle them, a decent respect to the opinions of mankind requires that they should declare the causes which impel them to the separation.

We hold these truths to be self-evident, that all men are created equal, that they are endowed by their Creator with certain unalienable Rights, that among these are Life, Liberty and the pursuit of Happiness.—That to secure these rights, Governments are instituted among Men, deriving their just powers from the consent of the governed, —That whenever any Form of Government becomes destructive of these ends, it is the Right of the People to alter or to abolish it, and to institute new Government, laying its foundation on such principles and organizing its powers in such form, as to them shall seem most likely to effect their Safety and Happiness. Prudence, indeed, will dictate that Governments long established should not be changed for light and transient causes; and accordingly all experience hath shewn, that mankind are more disposed to suffer, while evils are sufferable, than to right themselves by abolishing the forms to which they are accustomed. But when a long train of abuses and usurpations, pursuing invariably

the same Object evinces a design to reduce them under abso-
lute Despotism, it is their right, it is their duty, to throw off such
Government, and to provide new Guards for their future security.
ÂSuch has been the patient sufferance of these Colonies; and such
is now the necessity which constrains them to alter their former
Systems of Government. The history of the present King of Great
Britain is a history of repeated injuries and usurpations, all having
in direct object the establishment of an absolute Tyranny over these
States. To prove this, let Facts be submitted to a candid world.

He has refused his Assent to Laws, the most wholesome and
necessary for the public good.

He has forbidden his Governors to pass Laws of immedi-
ate and pressing importance, unless suspended in their
operation till his Assent should be obtained; and when so
suspended, he has utterly neglected to attend to them.

He has refused to pass other Laws for the accommodation
of large districts of people, unless those people would relin-
quish the right of Representation in the Legislature, a right
inestimable to them and formidable to tyrants only.

He has called together legislative bodies at places unusual,
uncomfortable, and distant from the depository of their
public Records, for the sole purpose of fatiguing them into
compliance with his measures.

He has dissolved Representative Houses repeatedly, for
opposing with manly firmness his invasions on the rights
of the people.

He has refused for a long time, after such dissolutions, to
cause others to be elected; whereby the Legislative powers,
incapable of Annihilation, have returned to the People at
large for their exercise; the State remaining in the mean time
exposed to all the dangers of invasion from without, and
convulsions within.

He has endeavoured to prevent the population of these States;
for that purpose obstructing the Laws for Naturalization
of Foreigners; refusing to pass others to encourage their
migrations hither, and raising the conditions of new
Appropriations of Lands.

He has obstructed the Administration of Justice, by refusing his Assent to Laws for establishing Judiciary powers.

He has made Judges dependent on his Will alone, for the tenure of their offices, and the amount and payment of their salaries.

He has erected a multitude of New Offices, and sent hither swarms of Officers to harrass our people, and eat out their substance.

He has kept among us, in times of peace, Standing Armies without the Consent of our legislatures.

He has affected to render the Military independent of and superior to the Civil power.

He has combined with others to subject us to a jurisdiction foreign to our constitution, and unacknowledged by our laws; giving his Assent to their Acts of pretended Legislation:

For Quartering large bodies of armed troops among us:

For protecting them, by a mock Trial, from punishment for any Murders which they should commit on the Inhabitants of these States:

For cutting off our Trade with all parts of the world:

For imposing Taxes on us without our Consent:

For depriving us in many cases, of the benefits of Trial by Jury:

For transporting us beyond Seas to be tried for pretended offences.

For abolishing the free System of English Laws in a neighbouring Province, establishing therein an Arbitrary government, and enlarging its Boundaries so as to render it at once an example and fit instrument for introducing the same absolute rule into these Colonies:

For taking away our Charters, abolishing our most valuable Laws, and altering fundamentally the Forms of our Governments:

For suspending our own Legislatures, and declaring themselves invested with power to legislate for us in all cases whatsoever.

He has abdicated Government here, by declaring us out of his Protection and waging War against us.

He has plundered our seas, ravaged our Coasts, burnt our towns, and destroyed the lives of our people.

He is at this time transporting large Armies of foreign Mercenaries to compleat the works of death, desolation and tyranny, already begun with circumstances of Cruelty & perfidy scarcely paralleled in the most barbarous ages, and totally unworthy the Head of a civilized nation.

He has constrained our fellow Citizens taken Captive on the high Seas to bear Arms against their Country, to become the executioners of their friends and Brethren, or to fall themselves by their Hands.

He has excited domestic insurrections amongst us, and has endeavoured to bring on the inhabitants of our frontiers, the merciless Indian Savages, whose known rule of warfare, is an undistinguished destruction of all ages, sexes and conditions.

In every stage of these Oppressions We have Petitioned for Redress in the most humble terms: Our repeated Petitions have been answered only by repeated injury. A Prince whose character is thus marked by every act which may define a Tyrant, is unfit to be the ruler of a free people.

Nor have We been wanting in attentions to our Brittish brethren. We have warned them from time to time of attempts by their legislature to extend an unwarrantable jurisdiction over us. We have reminded them of the circumstances of our emigration and settlement here. We have appealed to their native justice and magnanimity, and we have conjured them by the ties of our common kindred to disavow these usurpations, which, would inevitably interrupt our connections and correspondence. They too have been deaf to the voice of justice and of consanguinity. We must, therefore, acquiesce in the necessity, which denounces our Separation, and hold them, as we hold the rest of mankind, Enemies in War, in Peace Friends.

We, therefore, the Representatives of the united States of America, in General Congress, Assembled, appealing to the Supreme Judge of the world for the rectitude of our intentions, do, in the Name, and by Authority of the good People of these Colonies, solemnly publish and declare, That these United Colonies are, and of Right ought to be Free and Independent States; that they are Absolved from all Allegiance to the British Crown, and that all political connection between them and the State of Great Britain, is and ought to be totally dissolved; and that as Free and Independent States, they have full Power to levy War, conclude Peace, contract Alliances, establish Commerce, and to do all other Acts and Things which Independent States may of right do. And for the support of this Declaration, with a firm reliance on the protection of divine Providence, we mutually pledge to each other our Lives, our Fortunes and our sacred Honor.

Preamble and Bill of Rights of the U.S. Constitution

We the People of the United States, in Order to form a more perfect Union, establish Justice, insure domestic Tranquility, provide for the common defence, promote the general Welfare, and secure the Blessings of Liberty to ourselves and our Posterity, do ordain and establish this Constitution for the United States of America.

Amendment I
Congress shall make no law respecting an establishment of religion, or prohibiting the free exercise thereof; or abridging the freedom of speech, or of the press; or the right of the people peaceably to assemble, and to petition the Government for a redress of grievances.

Amendment II
A well regulated Militia, being necessary to the security of a free State, the right of the people to keep and bear Arms, shall not be infringed.

Amendment III
No Soldier shall, in time of peace be quartered in any house, without the consent of the Owner, nor in time of war, but in a manner to be prescribed by law.

Amendment IV
The right of the people to be secure in their persons, houses, papers, and effects, against unreasonable searches and seizures, shall not be violated, and no Warrants shall issue, but upon probable cause, supported by Oath or affirmation, and particularly describing the place to be searched, and the persons or things to be seized.

Amendment V
No person shall be held to answer for a capital, or otherwise infamous crime, unless on a presentment or indictment of a Grand Jury, except in cases arising in the land or naval forces, or in the Militia, when in actual service in time of War or public danger; nor shall any person be subject for the same offence to be twice put in jeopardy of life or limb; nor shall be compelled in any criminal case to be a witness against himself, nor be deprived of life, liberty, or property, without due process of law; nor shall private property be taken for public use, without just compensation.

Amendment VI
In all criminal prosecutions, the accused shall enjoy the right to a speedy and public trial, by an impartial jury of the State and district wherein the crime shall have been committed, which district shall have been previously ascertained by law, and to be informed of the nature and cause of the accusation; to be confronted with the witnesses against him; to have compulsory process for obtaining witnesses in his favor, and to have the Assistance of Counsel for his defence.

Amendment VII
In Suits at common law, where the value in controversy shall exceed twenty dollars, the right of trial by jury shall be preserved, and no fact tried by a jury, shall be otherwise re-examined in any Court of the United States, than according to the rules of the common law.

Amendment VIII
Excessive bail shall not be required, nor excessive fines imposed, nor cruel and unusual punishments inflicted.

Amendment IX
The enumeration in the Constitution, of certain rights, shall not be construed to deny or disparage others retained by the people.

Amendment X
The powers not delegated to the United States by the Constitution, nor prohibited by it to the States, are reserved to the States respectively, or to the people.

Stephen Williams attended the University of California at Berkeley on a swimming scholarship and graduated with a degree in economics. He worked as an economic consultant before pursuing a teaching career. Stephen spent ten years teaching 5th and 6th grade in the Cupertino Union School District in California.

Stephen founded Prepare the Way Ministries in 2006, following his involvement in a federal court case concerning the censorship of historical documents with Christian references. His principal and school district censored primary source documents including the *Declaration of Independence,* William Penn's *Frame of Government,* and Samuel Adams's *The Rights of the Colonists* due to their misinterpretation of the "separation of church and state." With the help of the legal firm Alliance Defending Freedom, Stephen filed a federal court case in November of 2004 to protect the freedom of speech and religion in public schools. The case gained national media attention, with TV interviews on Fox News and articles appearing in major newspapers. The case was settled out of court in the summer of 2005 and a written settlement was put in place that allowed primary source documents with Christian references to be used in Cupertino classrooms.

Having been on the front lines in the church/state battle, Stephen offers a unique perspective on the ways our culture can erode a Biblical worldview. Stephen speaks nationally on worldview, apologetics, and cultural issues, including navigating public schools as a Christian. He currently resides in Bend, Oregon with his family.

Sarah Williams completed a Ph.D. in environmental engineering with an emphasis in microbiology from Stanford University. She is the recipient of a National Science Foundation graduate fellowship. Prior to attending Stanford, Sarah graduated from the University of Michigan with a B.S. in engineering. While at the University of Michigan, she was awarded several Hopwood Awards in Poetry and Fiction; following her undergraduate coursework, Sarah was awarded a one-year fellowship to study English at Oxford University. She has published several scientific papers and book chapters in the area of environmental microbiology, as well as poems and stories in several magazines. She is married to Stephen Williams and is the mother of four daughters. She also consults part-time in the area of environmental engineering, enjoys creative writing, and helps with Prepare the Way Ministries.

Prepare the Way Ministries' Biblical Worldview Teaching Curriculum: Standing Firm

The Standing Firm curriculum package includes over six hours of teaching on four DVDs, discussion questions, an extended reading list, optional homework assignments, and Powerpoint slides.[1]

Outline of material covered

Part 1: What's the Problem?

- Are Christians ready to give a logical defense of the Christian faith to non-believers?
- Why are over 50% of Christian youth walking away from their faith when they leave home?

Part 2: The Reliability of Scripture

- Why is the Bible the most reliable document of antiquity? (Bibliographic Evidence)
- How do we know it is historically accurate? (External Evidence)
- Were the authors of the Bible eyewitnesses and accurate? (Internal Evidence)

---

[1] www.preparetheway.us/Resources/worldviewseminarteachingcurriculums

Part 3: Post-Modernism & Worldviews

- What is a worldview and why does it matter?
- Why is a Christian worldview the most rational, reasonable, and logical?

Part 4: Historical Revisionism

- How is our history being changed?
- Why is revisionist history a major stumbling block?

Part 5: Science and Christianity

- Are science and Christianity compatible?
- Why is Darwinian evolution a religion and how does it undermine a Christian worldview?

Part 6: Godly Sexuality

- How has today's sex-saturated society impacted Christians?
- Why is it critical for believers to remain pure?

Part 7: Influencing Culture

- How can Christians impact their spheres of influence in schools, workplaces, communities and culture; who is God calling to be His hands and feet?

To get the Biblical Worldview Teaching Curriculum *Standing Firm*, please visit our webpage (www.PrepareTheWay.us) and click on the Resources tab.

PREPARE THE WAY

The crooked roads shall become straight. the rough ways smooth.

LUKE 3:5

Equipping and empowering Christians to uphold a Biblical worldview and engage an increasingly secular culture.

Offering a variety of seminars and speaking topics that will help Christians live out their faith.[1]

We currently offer four main seminars:

1. Standing Firm—Empowering Christians with apologetic evangelism
2. America at a Crossroads—Learn about America's heritage and how to influence culture
3. Navigating Public Schools—Charting a course to protect a Christian worldview and live it out in public schools
4. Leading with a Pure Heart—Empowering men in the area of purity and leadership

Each seminar can be given as a 30-minute overview or a multi-session, in-depth series.

Contact us for more information and to schedule a seminar at your church, group, or organization.

American Heritage Sermon Series:

1. July 4th: A Celebration of History
2. Thanksgiving: A Uniquely American Holiday
3. President's Day: The Faith of Our Founders
4. National Day of Prayer: The Power of Prayer in Our Nation's History

Invite Stephen to preach at your church about one of these uniquely American holidays.

www.PrepareTheWay.us

---

[1] www.preparetheway.us/Speaking-Topics